MEDITATE

SUNY Series in Transpersonal and
Humanistic Psychology
Richard D. Mann and Jean B. Mann, Editors

Swami Muktananda
MEDITATE

SECOND EDITION WITH A CHAPTER BY
Gurumayi Chidvilasananda

State University of New York Press

Published by
State University of New York Press, Albany

Second Edition

Design by Kathie Kemp
Cover photograph by Gadhekar

For information, address State University of New York
Press, State University Plaza, Albany, N.Y. 12246

Library of Congress Cataloging in Publication Data

Muktananda, Swami, 1908–
Meditate / Swami Muktananda : with a chapter by
Gurumayi Chidvilasananda,—2nd ed.
p. cm.—(SUNY series in transpersonal and humanistic psychology)
Includes bibliographical references and index.
ISBN 0–7914–0978–3 (alk. paper)
1. Meditation. I. Chidvilasananda, Gurumayi. II. Title.
III. Series.
BL627.M84, 1991
294.5'43—dc20
91–3641
CIP

10 9 8 7 6 5 4 3 2 1

CONTENTS

SWAMI MUKTANANDA

And The Siddha Lineage

Swami Muktananda

Swami Muktananda was born in 1908, and from earliest childhood was fascinated by stories of the sages and saints. His parents lived near the South Indian city of Mangalore, and holy men often came to their home. When he was still a schoolboy, he met Bhagawan Nityananda, the ecstatic saint whom he would later recognize as his Master. Soon afterward, the boy was overcome by an intense desire for a direct experience of the Truth. And so, at the age of fifteen, he left home to begin a life of seeking. He went first to the ashram of a great Siddha Master named Siddharudha Swami. There he took initiation into *sannyasa*, or monkhood, receiving the name Swami Muktananda, which means the "bliss of liberation." For the next thirty years he traveled the length and breadth of India, searching for the Master who could give him the experience of God. He met over sixty great beings and learned much from them. He mastered the scriptures and became proficient in hatha yoga, Ayurvedic medicine, and other arts. Completely dedicated to his search, he underwent considerable difficulties and hardships, often going without food and shelter.

But the Truth he sought eluded him—until he came to the feet of the great Siddha Master whom he had met so many years before. Bhagawan Nityananda was an austere, utterly detached, overwhelmingly powerful being in whose presence all became silent. Recognizing him as the Guru he had sought, Swami Muktananda devoted himself to a life of discipleship. From Bhagawan Nityananda he received Shaktipat, the sacred initiation of the Siddha tradition, which awakened his inner Kundalini energy.

This began a nine-year period of intense internal transformation during which Swami Muktananda passed through all the stages of meditation. In 1956, he reached the culmination of his years of

Bhagawan Nityananda

practice, attaining the state of Self-realization. Still, he continued to live as a simple disciple in Ganeshpuri, the small village where his Guru had settled. Then, in 1961, Bhagawan Nityananda took *mahasamadhi*—the scriptural term for the passing of a saint. Before leaving the world, he transmitted the power of the Siddha lineage to Swami Muktananda, investing him with the full potency of his own tremendous spiritual attainment.

During the next few years, increasing numbers of spiritual seekers found their way to Swami Muktananda's ashram near Ganeshpuri. Among them were Europeans and Americans, Australians and Japanese, and soon they were inviting him to visit their countries. Baba, as he came to be known, made his first trip abroad in 1970. This was the beginning of a remarkable worldwide mission. During three successive tours of the West, he ignited the fire of meditation in hundreds of thousands of people. Empowered by his Guru to give Shaktipat initiation, Baba Muktananda awakened unprecedented numbers of people, of all ages and backgrounds, to the experience of their own inner divinity. Even people with little apparent interest in spirituality found themselves drawn by his love and attracted by the peace and power they felt in his presence.

Admired by artists and statesmen, sought out by writers and thinkers and other spiritual teachers, Baba was recognized as a figure of truly universal stature. His influence was enormous—so much so that he came to be called "the Guru's Guru." His teaching inspired people to live a life which supports the inner search, influencing thousands to look for strength and happiness within their own hearts.

During the 1970s many residential ashrams and centers for the practice of Siddha Yoga were founded, including the main SYDA Foundation ashram in the Catskill Mountains in New York State. Baba wrote and published over thirty books, established courses in yoga philosophy, and created the Siddha Meditation Intensive, during which he transmitted Shaktipat.

Gurumayi Chidvilasananda

For many years Baba trained his successor, Gurumayi Chidvilasananda. She first met him as a child of five. The loving bond of Guru and disciple was instantaneously formed, and from that time on, her development was closely supervised by Baba. Later, when he made his tours of the West, Gurumayi traveled with him, serving him in innumerable ways. She translated into English his writings, as well as his lectures and the many impromptu question-and-answer sessions that he held.

In 1982, these years of rigorous training culminated when Baba bequeathed to her the full power and knowledge of the Siddha lineage, the vast spiritual legacy which his own Guru had passed on to him. A few months later, Baba Muktananda took mahasamadhi, merging into the ultimate state of union with the Absolute.

When Gurumayi was still a young girl, Baba said of her, "She is a great flame. One day she will illumine the world." Now, as the Master of the Siddha lineage, Gurumayi bestows the treasured gift of Shaktipat, awakening the inner energy of seekers of all nationalities. Under her guidance, the Siddha Yoga ashrams and meditation centers around the world are thriving wellsprings of spiritual life and classical yogic wisdom.

As Gurumayi travels the world, thousands of people come to meet her at public programs. Through her own joyous example she shows us how to welcome others with respect and love. Above all, in her presence the awareness of our own inner divinity can be spontaneously ignited. Once that happens, we are able to perceive that same radiant divinity everywhere.

Through the living Master Gurumayi Chidvilasananda, the spiritual power and compassion of this great Siddha tradition continue to flourish in the world.

FOREWORD

This book is a specific and practical how-to primer of meditation, a "primary research manual" as one psychologist called it. But it is more than an outline of a method. It is itself a meditation experience when read with a certain open detachment and sense of venture.

Swami Muktananda, the author of this volume, is a Siddha. In his own country and tradition, the term "Siddha" indicates common acknowledgement that he has realized the Self, achieved the highest possible level of awareness and development. The criteria from which such a judgment is made have evolved over many thousands of years, and relatively few such Siddhas exist in any generation. Just as a mathematical genius stands at a sharp contrast to most of us in number-thinking, a Siddha, although he may look quite ordinary, has developed far beyond our ordinary abilities, mental processes, and awareness. The bestowal of the term "Siddha" is purely pragmatic. A Siddha must clearly demonstrate his Self-realization, not merely assert it. He has reached his state through a long process of meditation and inner inquiry and has developed the power to pass on to others the experience of meditation.

In other words, a true Siddha has the ability to initiate in others a spiritual process, not merely to inspire but to propel them toward the development of their own highest potential. Meditation is the means by which this development takes place. But meditation as a Siddha teaches it is very different from the various stress reduction techniques which we have grown to accept as meditation. In fact, according to Muktananda, stress reduction is only a byproduct of meditation, which is aimed at a much more far-reaching goal.

In these pages Muktananda writes: "We do not meditate to relax a little and experience some peace; we meditate to unfold our

3

inner being." What is this thing called the inner being, or inner Self as Muktananda usually refers to it? As I see it, the inner Self can be considered a kind of fourth dimension of our mind-brain-body system. It is the spiritual dimension, the consciousness within us which lies beyond verbal thought and which many of us glimpse at some point in our lives—perhaps at a moment of intense joy—and recognize as our highest Self, the part of us that remains outside fear, anger, and the other psychic detritus that normally cloud our consciousness.

If we think about it, we realize that many aspects of human development from conception to maturity are designed to bring us to awareness of our functional unity with this inner Self. Unfortunately, most aspects of culture seem equally designed to sidetrack or derail this natural development. Ours is an anxiety culture, and once we have become acculturated, that anxiety manifests in our life in infinite ways. We are seduced into trying to cope with or treat anxiety's manifestations, without recognizing the cause. According to the Eastern analysis, there is but one root cause of anxiety—no matter how varied its branchings—and that is separation from the inner Self. This is what Siddha Meditation is designed to remedy because, ultimately, connection with the Self is the only thing which can give us real happiness, strength, freedom, and the ability to connect wholly with others. For this reason, philosophers and mystics of all cultures have argued that only when we live in contact with that Self can we be considered to have matured as human beings. In fact, Muktananda, along with the philosophers of his own tradition, insists that the inner Self is identical with God, the highest truth, and states that to discover this Self within is actually the goal of human life.

Meditation, as he teaches it, is the process through which one can eventually come to experience one's identity with this inner Self, or inner God. Meditation, Muktananda tells us, is easy, natural, and spontaneous. Early in this manual he points out that virtually every activity of our day-to-day life involves some form of concentration. The only difference between this form of "meditation" and meditation on the inner Self is that we focus our attention inside rather than on some particular activity. Once that initial shift of focus is made, meditation happens very naturally. In fact, according to Muktananda, such meditation is not an activity one performs but a state one slips into, much as one slips into sleep. It is not a matter of technique but of knowledge and understanding. Therefore, his guide to meditation does not present a rigid method. Instead, it establishes an atmosphere in which meditation can take place.

One of the metaphors Muktananda often uses when he discusses meditation is that of the four wheels of a car. The wheels are the practices, or in some cases the mental attitudes, that the meditator uses to support the vehicle of meditation and carry it forward. They are vitally important, but they should not be mistaken for the car itself. In other words, the practices are not in themselves the process, but are rather the supports one needs in order to allow the process to take place and to keep it going.

The first wheel of meditation is awareness of, or focus on, the object of meditation. As already stated, Muktananda maintains that the target of Siddha Meditation is nothing less than the highest truth, God, which can be experienced as our own Self. Just as Jesus said, "The kingdom of God is within you," he maintains that God can be found only within our own hearts, and that not until we become one-pointed on this awareness do our efforts at meditation take us in the right direction.

In discussing the object of meditation, Muktananda also mentions the mind, which most meditators find to be the major distraction or obstacle in their practice. By the mind, he is referring here to our endless stream of mental chatter. He has several prescriptions for dealing with this thought stream, but his essential point is that if the meditator is clear about the goal of meditation and focuses on it, the mind will take care of itself. Here Muktananda delivers one of his most radical and, for a beginner in meditation, most valuable prescriptions. He explains that the mind is, in fact, nothing but a form of universal consciousness with a tendency to congeal into thoughts or images. If one regards it as consciousness rather than considering it a barrier or allowing oneself to be seduced by the thoughts and images it projects, it will no longer be a problem.

To provide a point of focus for the mind's tendency to construct thoughts and images, Muktananda adds the second wheel of the meditation car: mantra. A mantra is a word or sound that serves as an object of concentration and thus harnesses the mental energy that ordinarily becomes scattered in random thinking. Moreover, according to Muktananda, a mantra given by a living Guru is nothing less than "a vibration of the Self; it is the true speech of the Self, and when we immerse ourselves in it, it takes us to the place of the Self."

It may be difficult for Westerners to accept Muktananda's teaching that "mantra is God." ("There is no difference," he writes, "between God and His name; mantra has all the powers of God.") The biblical injunction that the name of God is sacrosanct and filled with power, or the teaching of Jesus that we are judged by every word that comes out of our mouth, since the Word is creation—is no longer meaningful to a people satiated with broadcast and printed words. And yet the power of words is attested to by numerous experimenters as well as by our commonsense observations. In the beginning *is* the word. As Northrop Frye expressed it, "The word lifts order out of chaos."

The basis of Muktananda's use of mantra is the ancient notion, now beginning to be backed up by contemporary sound wave research, that certain vibratory patterns of sound can bridge the gap between surface thinking and the consciousness which underlies all reality—that is, between our personal awareness and the Self within us. Certain forms of energy do resonate with other forms of energy, and when this resonance occurs, the word, or mantra, can function to align the mind of the meditator with the subtle consciousness of the inner Self.

The third wheel mentioned by Muktananda is *asana*, Sanskrit for the bodily position we assume for meditation. We must quiet the body in order to quiet the mental chatter. Asana is a position which reduces muscular movement to a minimum. Assuming the same position every time we meditate, and holding that position, is the foundation on which meditation rests. Whole patterns of automatic brain responses are locked into our various body positions and gestures. In fact, our ordinary life is made up of a repertoire of personal gestures which keep intact the repetitive patterns of thought and perception that make up our personality. This tendency of the body to form habit-patterns is utilized on behalf of meditation; Muktananda says that when we always adopt a certain position for meditation, it helps us get into meditation.

The fourth wheel is breath. Muktananda insists on a perfectly natural breath. One of the fundamental principles of meditation is that the mind and the breath are linked and that when the breathing is allowed to become quiet by itself, the mind will naturally become quiet. To help in establishing this link, Muktananda suggests combining the mantra with the breathing process.

These, then, are the four wheels of Muktananda's meditation car. However, it is when we come to the question of what keeps the car running that we confront the unique aspect of Siddha Meditation. This meditation process, Muktananda says, really begins with the awakening of a subtle inner energy which is known in Sanskrit as "Shakti" and is said to lie dormant in everyone. Until this energy is awakened, meditation depends entirely on one's own effort and willpower and is, therefore, more or less difficult. Every beginning meditator knows how boring and uncomfortable the process of focusing inward can be. But the awakening of this energy makes meditation a different matter: Once activated, it fuels meditation and propels the meditator toward a connection with the Self.

According to the texts of the Siddha tradition, the easiest way to activate this inner energy is through contact with a person who has fully developed it in himself. This is one of the first issues

Muktananda deals with, since it is one of the first steps in Siddha Meditation. "When the Guru's power is transmitted into us and awakens our own dormant power," Muktananda explains, "meditation comes to us spontaneously, on its own."

Here our Western orientation may bog down on several levels. For one thing, the term "Guru" is a troubled word in our time. "Guru" is Sanskrit for "dark to light" and means, quite simply, a teacher and/or teaching principle that leads us from the darkness of ignorance to the light of knowledge. (The Latin word *educare*, from which we get the word "education," means the same thing.) However, it is important to note that knowledge here refers not to acquired information but to direct perceptual experience of a subtler level of reality than we ordinarily see. Knowledge of the Self requires precisely that sort of subtle perception, because it is simply not accessible to our ordinary modes of thinking or sensory awareness.

The principal function of the Guru in Siddha Meditation is to transmit spiritual energy and initiate the student's development of it.* This is said to be the specific initial act of leading the student from darkness to light, from ignorance to knowledge. Eastern texts refer to this initiation as "Shaktipat," the awakening of spiritual power. Once this power is awakened, Muktananda says, knowledge in the form of direct perceptual awareness arises spontaneously and, developed through meditation, leads sooner or later to the experience of the Self.

It should be noted that the principles outlined in this study are classical principles of yoga, that comprehensive system for developing the mind, body, and spirit which is one of the East's great contributions to human psychology. Muktananda's background is in this tradition, and the texts of the Indian spiritual culture form

---

*The activation of the inner energy which the Guru brings about can happen through personal contact with him, through contact with one of his disciples, or through other, more subtle means. My own initial experience in Siddha Meditation actually occurred while I was reading one of Muktananda's books.—J.C.P.

the whole basis of his thought. Surprising correlations are being found between physics, brain research, biology, and the ancient Vedantic and Kashmir Shaivite texts that furnish the textual background of Siddha Meditation. Muktananda teaches by a multilevel approach that is often challenging to our Western linear logic. But never is there any suggestion of the nonrational or alogical. Muktananda is not out to trick our minds or outmaneuver our reasoning. Nothing in his teaching is intentionally obscure, paradoxical, or cryptic. Nonetheless, he addresses us in a way that forces our ordinary logic either to expand with him or to retire. The reader is urged to twist the tiger's tail a bit here and there and risk expansion, even into the experience of "finding God in the heart."

Muktananda closes this book with a brief account of Siddha Meditation in general, dwelling particularly on the absolutely unqualified, total nature of the goal he knows himself and desires for each of us: our own personal unity with God. I am reminded of my favorite couplet from William Blake:

More! More! is the cry of a mistaken soul:
Less than All cannot satisfy man.

The wonder and beauty of Muktananda's teaching is his awareness that we must indeed have All, that nothing less than our absolute unity with God can ever satisfy, that our substitutes fail, turn on us, and destroy us. To this end, Muktananda presents his four-wheeled car of meditation, powered by his grace and strength and designed to carry us to the goal of all desire—"that region of the heart wherein God lives."

This revised edition of the classic, MEDITATE, ends with a talk "Looking Within," by Gurumayi Chidvilasananda. Muktananda trained Gurumayi in the Siddha tradition and then passed to her, as her own living state, the totality of his universal power. Our fortune and joy is that she now stands ready to pass this on to all who come to her willing to receive what she has to give.

"Look within," Gurumayi urges us. "Meditate...find your own treasure." What she offers us, she claims, is only our own being.

As with Muktananda we find that Gurumayi's words carry the extraordinary power and eloquence of her presence. These pages then are yet another avenue of grace, another means to be in the presence of a Siddha.

Joseph Chilton Pearce

MEDITATE

Meditate on the Self

In the Upanishads there is a question: What do human beings want? The answer is that we want happiness. Everything we do, we do for the sake of happiness. We seek that happiness through our work, through our friends and family, through art and science, through food, drink, and entertainment. For happiness, we perform all the activities of daily life, and this is why we keep expanding our material world.

Inside us lies divine happiness, the same happiness we are looking for in the world. If we think about the joy we derive from different activities, we will realize that we experience happiness not in the activities, but within ourselves. For example, when you look at a beautiful picture, where do you feel pleasure, in the picture or in yourself? When you eat a delicious meal, do you experience satisfaction in the food or in yourself? When you meet a friend and feel joy, is that joy in your friend or in yourself? The truth is that the joy you find in all these things is simply a reflection of the joy of your own inner Self.

The testimony for this is our sleep. At the end of every day, no matter how much we have eaten or drunk or earned or enjoyed, we are exhausted. All we want to do is to go into our bedroom, turn off the light, and take refuge in a blanket. During sleep, we are completely alone. We do not want our wife, our husband, our friends, our possessions. We do not eat anything, we do not earn anything, we do not enjoy anything. Yet, while we are sleeping, the weariness of our waking hours is removed independently, by the strength of our own spirit. In the morning, when we wake up, we feel completely rested.

This is an experience that we have every day. If we think carefully about why we become exhausted from everything we do during the day and why we get so much peace from sleep, we will understand that the real source of our contentment is not eating or drinking or anything outside ourselves, but is within. During the day, the mind turns outward. However in the sleep state, the mind takes some rest in the Self, and it is this which removes our fatigue. Absorbed in the little bliss of sleep, we forget the pains of the waking state. If we were to go just beyond sleep and enter into the state of meditation, we would be able to drink the nectar of love and happiness which lies in the heart.

That nectar is what we are looking for in all the activities of the outer world. What we are really seeking is the supreme Truth, and through meditation we can experience that Truth vibrating in the form of sublime happiness in the heart.

Truly speaking, a human being is divine. It is only our wrong understanding which keeps us small. We think of ourselves as the body. We think that we are a certain physical structure, with hands, feet, legs, and eyes. We think of ourselves as a man or a woman, as belonging to a particular class or country. We identify ourselves with our thoughts, our talents, our good or bad actions. But none of these things is what we are.

Within us is a being who knows all the actions of the body and the mind and remains untouched by all of them. In the *Bhagavad Gita*, Lord Krishna says:

idam shariram kaunteya kshetramityabhidhiyate;
etadyo vetti tam prahuh kshetrajna iti tadvidah.

> Arjuna, this body is called a field, and the one who knows it is called the knower of the field.[1]

The one who knows the field must be different from the field. For example, one who says "my book" must be different from the book; one who says "my table" must be different from the table. In the same way, one who says "my body" must be different from the body; one who says "my mind" must be different from the mind.

Who is that being who observes the activities of our waking hours? At night, when we go to sleep, that being does not sleep, but stays awake and in the morning reports to us on our dreams. Who is that knower? In the *Gita*, Krishna answers this question: *kshetrajnam chapi mam viddhi sarvakshetreshu bharata*, O Arjuna, I am the knower of all these fields.[2]

The one who lives in the body but who is apart from the body as the knower of it is our real Self. That Self is beyond the body, beyond the mind, beyond distinctions of name, color, and sex. It is the pure "I," the original "I"-consciousness which has been with us since we came into the world. We have superimposed different notions onto that "I"-awareness, notions like, "I am black," "I am white," "I am a man," "I am a woman," "I am American," "I am Indian." Yet, when we wipe away those superimpositions, that "I" is nothing but pure Consciousness, and it is of the form of bliss. It was with the awareness of that "I" that the great Shankaracharya proclaimed, *Aham Brahmasmi*, "I am the Absolute."[3] That "I" is God, and we meditate to know that directly. As we see it more and more, we become transformed.

There are many techniques which are supposed to lead us to God, but of all these, meditation is the one recognized by all the saints and sages, because only in meditation can we see the inner Self directly. That which lives in the heart cannot be found in books. If we look for it in churches and temples, we cannot find it. Logical reasoning and the ability to give great lectures are of no use either. Since that being is our innermost Consciousness, it is necessary for us to turn within to have a direct experience of it.

There was a time when I was addicted to reading the scriptures. One day I went to see my Guru with a book under my arm. He said, "Muktananda, come here. What is that?"

"It's an Upanishad," I replied.

"Do you know how this book was made?" he asked me. "It was made by a brain. The brain may make any number of books, but a book cannot make a brain. You had better throw it away and meditate."

So I threw the book away and began to meditate. This makes perfect sense. When the Self is within, why should we look for knowledge of it somewhere else? As long as we do not realize the Self within, we cannot find true peace. We can never be happy, no matter how much we have in the outside world. So meditation has the highest importance; it is necessary for everyone.

The Upanishads say that everything in the universe is in meditation.[4] The earth is held in position by meditation, fire burns through the power of meditation, water flows through the power of meditation, and the wind blows through the power of meditation. Through meditation, the ancient sages discovered the various laws of society and how to govern so that everything functioned smoothly. In the same way, the secrets of the ancient sciences were revealed to these sages. Through meditation, they accomplished great tasks.

Meditation is universal. It is not the property of any particular sect or cult. It does not belong to the East or to the West, nor does it belong to Hinduism, Buddhism, or Sufism. Meditation is everyone's property, just as sleep is everyone's property: It belongs to humanity. Meditation is not something difficult or strange. All of us, in our daily lives, are already familiar with it. Without meditation, a doctor could not diagnose a disease, nor could a lawyer prepare a brief, nor a student pass an examination. All our arts and skills, from driving a car to cooking a meal to painting a picture to solving a mathematical problem, are perfected through the power of concentration, which is nothing but meditation. However, these are external forms of meditation. When we turn our attention within and focus on our inner being, just as we focus on external objects, we are meditating on the Self.

Meditation is such a great purifier that it washes away the sins of countless lifetimes and removes all the impurities and tensions which beset the mind. Meditation rids us of disease and makes us more skillful at everything we do. Through meditation, our inner awareness expands and our understanding of inner and outer things becomes steadily deeper. Through meditation, we travel to different inner worlds and have innumerable inner experiences.

Above all, meditation stills the mind—which constantly wanders, which constantly causes suffering—and establishes us forever in the state of supreme peace, which is independent of any external factors. Ultimately, meditation makes us aware of our own true nature. It is this awareness which removes all suffering and delusion, and this awareness comes only when we see, face to face, our own inner Self.

If, even once, we could see the Self as separate from the body, we would understand that the body does not bind us, that the pains and pleasures of the body do not affect us. According to the seers of Vedanta, pain and pleasure affect only a person who does not know the inner Self.[5] Even in daily life we know that we experience physical pain and pleasure only for a certain length of time and only in a certain state of Consciousness; we do not experience them at all times or in all states. For example, if a person has a boil on his hand, it hurts during the day, but as soon as he goes to sleep, he stops feeling the pain. A person may have a nightmare in which he sees a tiger rushing at him, and he may become frightened and scream, "Save me, save me!" But when he awakens, the tiger is nowhere around, and he realizes that he has only been dreaming.

So the pleasures and pains of the dream state do not reach the waking state. In the same way, the state of meditation is beyond the pleasures and pains of the waking, dream, and deep-sleep states. In meditation, we become the witness of all our states. This is the state of God, of the inner Self, and through meditation we can attain that state because it is within us. When we pass from dream to waking consciousness, our understanding of ourselves changes. In the same way, when we reach the state of the Self, we understand ourselves differently; we understand that we are divine.

There was a great being named Hazrit Bayazid Bistami. He was a Sufi who used to pray and meditate continually. As his meditation became deeper he reached a state in which he began to proclaim, "I am God, I am God." One who has not experienced that state may find it hard to understand, so I will explain with a simple analogy. You know from your own experience that your idea of yourself keeps changing as your consciousness changes. A policeman, as long as he is an ordinary policeman, will keep saying, "I am a policeman." When he becomes a captain, he will stop saying, "I am a policeman," and say, "I am a captain." And when he becomes a commissioner he will say, "I am a commissioner." As long as a person is studying, he says, "I am a student," but when he finishes his studies and begins to teach, he says, "I am a teacher." The same "I" is experiencing all these states. When that "I" which identifies itself with the body in the waking state, saying, "This body is mine," or "I am a policeman," or "I am an American," passes from the level of waking consciousness to the highest, subtlest level of consciousness, it attains this awareness: I am God. That understanding emanates from the deepest place inside us.

When a river flows into the ocean and becomes one with the ocean, it is no longer a river; it is the ocean. In the same way, Hazrit Bistami would reach a state in which he would experience himself as all-pervasive Consciousness, the highest Truth, and he would shout, "I am God." He did not know what was happening to him, and he could not pass into this state at will.

Although he was a great being, Bistami's teachings had always been the orthodox teachings of Muslim priests. He would tell his students, "Pray to God, be forgiven for your sins. God is somewhere up above." So when Bistami began to shout during meditation, "I am God, I am God," his students were shocked. When he came out of his room, they surrounded him and cried, "Bistami, you are guilty of a terrible heresy! We cannot understand what is happening."

Bistami said, "Please tell me, what sin have I committed?"

The students explained, "We could hear you exclaiming from inside your room, 'I am God, I am God.' How can a human being, who is corrupt and sinful, be God? That goes against the holy law of Islam."

"I am not really to blame for this," Bistami told them. "When I am in meditation, I am not in control of what I say. If you hear me say these things again, you can punish me in any way you like."

The students agreed. After about a week's time, Bistami again sat in meditation. This time he began to shout louder than ever, "I am God, I am God, I am God! This earth has come from me. I am the mountains and all the oceans. I flow as water in the rivers. I am everywhere. I am in the West and the East; I am in the North and the South; I am above and below."

When the students heard Bistami shouting in this way, they thought he had become completely insane and rushed to get weapons in order to silence him. As soon as Bistami came out of his room after meditation, the students grabbed him and began to beat him.

There was only one of him, and there were so many students. What could he do? So, once again, he sat down. The moment he touched the ground, he glided into meditation and began to proclaim, "I am God, I am God. Whatever there is has emanated from me. Fire cannot burn me, water cannot wet me, and bullets cannot kill me. I am in that state which is beyond everything. I am the highest of the high. Death cannot come anywhere near me. I am That which is the supreme Lord."

As the students were stoning and beating Bistami, an amazing thing happened. The punishment they were inflicting began to rebound onto themselves. The student who had been hitting Bistami's head found his own head being hit. The one who had struck his arms found his own arms hurt. Another who had been beating his legs found his own legs broken. Finally, for their own sake, the students stopped beating Bistami and sat down.

Bistami was still shouting, "I am God, I am God," but the students did not want to take another chance. They sat at a respectful distance, daring not to go anywhere near him. After a while Bistami came out of meditation, and the students said to him, "Sir, we don't understand what has happened. Our legs and arms are bleeding. Our heads are broken. We thought we were hitting you, but we ended up hitting ourselves."

Bistami said, "When I was in meditation, when I was in that state, I was no longer Bistami. I was the highest goal of your religion. I was all-pervasive, and, if anyone hits a being in such a state, it is like hitting one's own Self. That is why the blows bounced back onto you."

This is the state that we are supposed to attain in meditation. We do not meditate only to relax a little and experience some peace. We meditate to unfold our inner being. The *Brihajjabala Upanishad* says: Through meditation, we reach a place where the wind does not blow, where the heat of the sun does not reach, where death cannot penetrate.[6] This is the country of eternal bliss. If a yogi becomes established there, he becomes liberated. Death cannot touch him.

Shaktipat

Meditation on the Self is not difficult. The real secret of meditation is Shaktipat, the inner awakening that takes place through contact with a Siddha Guru. Within every human being lies a great and divine energy. The Indian scriptures refer to it by different names, such as Shakti (supreme energy) or Chiti (universal Consciousness), and when it resides within a human body, this conscious energy is known as Kundalini. This inner power is the same creative force which is responsible for the creation, sustenance, and withdrawal of the world. The *Pratyabhijnahridayam*, one of the essential texts of the great spiritual philosophy Kashmir Shaivism, describes this energy in an aphorism: *chitih svatantra vishva siddhi hethuhu*, Universal Consciousness creates this universe in total freedom.[7]

Contemporary scientists are becoming aware that the basis of the universe is energy. They are discovering what the sages of India have known for millennia: that it is Consciousness which forms the ground, or canvas, on which the material universe is drawn. In fact, the entire world is the play of this energy. Within its own being, by its own free will, it manifests this universe of diversities and becomes all the forms and shapes we see around us. This energy pervades every particle of the universe, from the supreme principle to the tiniest insect, and performs infinite functions. Yet, even though it becomes the world, this Consciousness remains untouched and free of stain.

Just as this energy pervades the universe, it permeates the human body, filling it from head to toe. It is this Shakti which carries on all our life functions. It becomes the *prana* and *apana*, the incoming and outgoing breaths. It is the power that makes our heart beat and causes the blood to flow in our veins. In this way, this conscious energy powers our bodies.

However, in its inner spiritual aspect, the energy ordinarily lies dormant. The awakening of this latent inner energy is essential for all of us, because only when it is activated and unfolds within us are we truly able to experience the Self.[8] This inner Kundalini Shakti resides at a subtle energy center known as the *muladhara chakra*, located at the base of the spine. The awakening of this energy is the beginning of a subtle inner process, leading ultimately to the state of union with the Self.

There are several ways this awakening can take place. However, the easiest is through Shaktipat, the transmission of energy from a fully Self-realized spiritual Master. In Shaktipat, just as a lit candle lights an unlit one, one's inner energy is kindled by the fully unfolded energy of the Guru. Then, one no longer has to make an effort to meditate. Meditation comes spontaneously on its own.

Knowledge

The Upanishads teach that we cannot attain the Self simply by doing good actions or by performing rituals. We can attain the Self only through direct knowledge;[9] it is that knowledge which makes us one with God. When our dormant Shakti is awakened, this knowledge arises very naturally, and we are able to see the Self.

If we had the right understanding, we could experience God right away. If the sun is out and we go outside, we see it immediately. How much time does it take to see the sun when it is shining in the sky?

In the same way, the light of God is shining within us all the time. How long should it take us to perceive that light which shines at every moment in our hearts? This is why the scriptures say that we meditate not to attain God, but to perceive the God who is already within us. Kashmir Shaivism says that if one does not already have something, trying to attain it is of no use, since one can lose it in the future. The *Vijnana Bhairava*, one of the revealed texts of Kashmir Shaivism, teaches that God, the Self, is present in all one's inner feelings, one's inner understanding, and one's inner knowledge.[10] He is closer than anyone or anything; it is only because of our weak understanding that we are not able to know Him.

The sage Vasishtha told Lord Rama, "It is very easy to see God. You can see Him in the time it takes to blink your eyes. Yet many life-times have gone by, and you still haven't seen Him."[11]

The Upanishads teach that God is of the form of *sat, chit,* and *ananda*: absolute existence, consciousness, and bliss. Sat means Truth, that which exists in all places, in all things, and at all times. If Truth were not omnipresent, it would not be the Truth; it would not have absolute existence. For example, if you are in New York, you are real in New York; but since you are not in Los Angeles, you are not real there. But God, being sat, is not bound by place or time, nor is He restricted to one particular object. What object is there which is not Shiva?[12] What country is there where Shiva is not? That Consciousness, that God, exists in His fullness in everything. Being present in everything, He is present in our hearts, and we can find Him there.

The next element is chit. Chit means Consciousness, or that which illuminates everything. Chit is the light of the Self, which destroys ignorance. Chit makes us aware of all outer objects, and it also makes us aware that God exists inside. Moreover if we think that God does not exist because we have not seen Him, it is chit which illuminates that understanding. Chit is the discloser of the knowledge that something exists or does not exist. Chit is that which illuminates all places and all things at all times; therefore, chit also illuminates our inner being.

The final element is ananda. Ananda is absolute bliss, the bliss of Consciousness. This bliss is far superior to the pleasure that arises from seeing a beautiful form, hearing a melodious sound, tasting delicious food, or experiencing the softness of a touch. The pleasure born of looking at a beautiful form depends on that form, and if the form disappears, the bliss also disappears. The pleasure which comes from listening to a melodious sound depends on that sound, and if the sound disappears, the pleasure also disappears. In the same way, the pleasure born of a soft touch depends on that touch, and when the touch is no more, the pleasure also dies. But ananda does not depend on any external factor. It arises, unconditioned, from within. When the mind and intellect come close to the Self, they are able to experience bliss. It is to attain that bliss, to establish ourselves in that bliss, that we meditate. When we attain the light of the Self within ourselves, that light emerges as supreme Love.

So God, the Self, is of the form of sat, chit, and ananda. Being sat, chit, and ananda, He pervades everywhere, and therefore we can see Him anywhere. The real question is, Do we want to see God as He is or as we want Him to be? If we want to see Him as He is, He is manifest; He is not concealed. If the intellect is sufficiently subtle and refined, we can experience Him instantly. This is why the sages agree that, in the attainment of the Self, understanding and knowledge are more important than techniques of meditation. Mere spiritual practice will not help us to know God. People think that by pursuing different practices they can attain Him. They take a course here and do not attain anything; they take a course there and do not attain anything. They take course after course, and the more expensive the course, the more they rush to enroll in it. However the object of spiritual practice, or *sadhana*, is not attained by these practices. Kashmir Shaivism speaks of the net of sadhana, and says that spiritual practices cannot illuminate the Self any more than a pot can illuminate the sun.[13]

Once Sheik Nasrudin woke up early in the morning. There was no moon; it was pitch-black. He called his disciple Mahmud and asked him to go outside and see if the sun had risen.

Mahmud went out, and came back a moment later. "O Nasrudin Sahib, it is very dark outside. I cannot see the sun at all."

"You idiot!" shouted Nasrudin. "Haven't you got the sense to use a flashlight?"

To expect a mere spiritual discipline to illuminate the indwelling God is like trying to see the sun with a flashlight. If the sun has really risen, one does not have to use a flashlight to see it. The flashlight cannot shine beside the sun, nor can darkness bear to remain after the sun has come up. In the same way, no technique can reveal the Self. Nothing can illuminate the Self, because it is the Self which illuminates everything.

It is only because our inner instruments are not refined enough to approach the Self that we have to meditate.[14] The *Yoga Sutras* of Patanjali, an authoritative scripture on meditation, explains that although the Self is always blazing within us, the restlessness of the mind acts as a barrier. According to Patanjali, when the mind becomes still and turns inward, we immediately perceive the Self.[15]

The Object of Meditation

The first question that arises when we sit for meditation is, On what should we meditate? People meditate on all kinds of objects and recommend many different techniques. Maharishi Patanjali speaks of concentration, or *dharana*, in which one focuses one's attention on a particular object in order to still and focus the mind.[16] One can concentrate on the heart, on the space between the eyebrows, or on other centers of the body. One can also focus on a being who has risen above passion and attachment; as the mind clings to such a being, it will take on his qualities. In fact, Patanjali says that one may concentrate wherever the mind finds satisfaction.

However, the best object of meditation is the inner Self. When the Self is the goal of meditation, why should we choose another object? If we want to experience the Self, we should meditate on the Self. If we want to know God, we should meditate on God. The mind becomes like that on which it meditates. The poet-saint Sundardas sang:

> *The mind which always thinks of a woman takes on a woman's form.*
> *The mind which is always angry burns in the fire of anger.*
> *The mind which contemplates illusion falls into the well of illusion.*
> *The mind which continually takes refuge in the Supreme*
>   *eventually becomes That.*

For this reason we should choose for the object of meditation that which is our true nature. When we meditate on the Self, not only do we experience the Self, we become the very form of the Self.

Once a seer asked a sage, "Who is that God on whom I can meditate?" The sage replied, "God is the witness of your mind." That witness is the goal of meditation. The Upanishads say, "It lives in the mind, but the mind cannot know it, because the mind is its body."[17] The Self is the witness of the mind, and it is also the source of the mind. In the *Kena Upanishad* there is a statement: "That is God who makes the mind think but who can never be apprehended by the mind."[18] One whom the mind can think about cannot be the supreme Truth, because that Self is the motive power behind all the movements of the mind. The Self makes the mind think, the imagination fantasize, and the ego constantly prattle, "I, I, I." In the same way, God is the one through whose inspiration we meditate.

In the *Gita*, Lord Krishna says:

sarvendriyagunabhasam sarvendriyavivarjitam;
asaktam sarvabhricchaiva nirgunam gunabhoktru cha.

O Arjuna, That shines through all our senses yet is without the senses. It supports all the senses yet remains apart
from them. It experiences the different qualities of nature yet
remains detached from them.[19]

Who is that being who knows all the positive and negative
thoughts which come and go in the mind? During meditation,
when we have inner problems, that being perceives all of them. That
being is of the form of knowledge. It is that which makes us know
everything. For example, in meditation, something comes up
inside. First, we become aware of it; we have the knowledge that it
is arising. Then, we know exactly what it is. We identify it as a good
or bad thought. That which makes us aware of the existence of
something, and of exactly what it is, is nothing but the Self. It is that
pure awareness which is the Self, not our good or our bad thoughts.
Within and without, whatever action takes place, whatever we do,
it is the Self that makes us aware that it is happening. This awareness is constantly there, inside us. It is the pure "I"-consciousness,
without form or attribute. Just as it knows everything inside and outside, it knows itself. To know this knower is true meditation.

How to Deal with the Mind

The highest meditation is the state of complete inner stillness.
In that state, not a single thought arises in the mind. However most
people cannot attain this state of stillness right away. For that reason, it is of the greatest importance for a meditator to understand
how to deal with the mind.

Most people who meditate make the same mistake. When they
sit for meditation they do not focus on the Self. Instead, they run
after the mind, trying to find out what it is doing. People always
complain to me, "When I try to meditate, different thoughts keep

rushing into my mind." Sometimes their minds are filled with anger, sometimes with hatred, sometimes with lust. At one moment, they are thinking of someone they love; at another moment, they are remembering their past bad actions and are filled with remorse. The more they try to obliterate thoughts from the mind, the more thoughts rush in. Instead of meditating on the Self, they find themselves like the seeker who found himself meditating on a monkey.

Once there was a seeker who went to a Guru to learn meditation. The Guru said, "I will choose an auspicious time for your initiation, and then I will call you." When the auspicious hour came, the Guru called the seeker and made all the proper arrangements for the initiation. After he had completed all the parts of the ritual, he said, "I am going to give you an important instruction. When you sit for meditation, first bow in all four directions and begin to repeat your mantra. But remember one thing. Whatever you do, don't think of a monkey."

"Why on earth would I think of a monkey?" asked the disciple. "I never thought of a monkey in my life. I don't care about monkeys; I care only about God."

When the initiation was over the young man returned home, spread out a mat, and sat on it, facing east. He took a sip of holy water and bowed in all four directions, and then he began to think about his Guru's last instruction. "What was it my Guru said? Oh, yes, 'Don't think of a monkey.'" Immediately a monkey appeared in his mind.

The seeker was upset. "Where did that monkey come from?" he wondered. He opened his eyes and took another sip of holy water. Again, he recalled what his Guru had said: "Don't think of a monkey." Once again, a monkey stood before him.

The seeker made three, four, five more attempts to meditate and each time was confronted with the monkey. Finally, he rushed back to his Guru. "O Guru, O holy seer, what shall I do? Until I came to you I didn't know what a monkey looked like, and now, when I sit for meditation, a monkey is all I can see."

This is what happens when we try to subdue the mind forcibly in meditation. Instead of worrying about the thoughts in the mind, instead of trying to erase the thoughts from the mind, it would be much better if we tried to understand the nature of the mind. What is the mind? The mind has no independent existence. The Upanishads say that the Self has itself become the mind.[20] The mind is nothing but a contracted form of the supreme Consciousness that has created the universe. The *Pratyabhijnahridayam* explains this in an aphorism: *chitireva chetana padadavarudha chetya sankochini chittam*.[21] This means that, when Consciousness descends from its status as pure Consciousness and assumes limitations, it becomes the stuff of the mind.

This is easy to understand if we think about what actually comprises the thoughts and images of the mind. The horse, the dog, and the camel that arise in the mind are not made of anything material; they are made of Consciousness. The aphorism says that the mind-stuff which forms itself into a camel, a dog, or a horse is nothing but a pulsation of the same Consciousness which has formed the universe. Another aphorism in the *Pratyabhijnahridayam* is: *svecchaya svabittau vishvam unmilayati*,[22] which means that Consciousness, that divine energy, has created the universe out of its own being, without taking the help of anything outside itself. In the same way, when Consciousness becomes the mind by assuming limitations, it begins to create endless mental universes. There are many outer universes, but they are all contained in Consciousness. In the same way, the universes that vibrate in the mind should not be seen as different from Consciousness. If you can look at your mind in this way, you will have very good meditation.

Let your mind spin as much as it wants to; do not try to subdue it. Simply witness the different thoughts as they arise and subside. No matter what thoughts and images arise in the mind, be aware that there is no concrete material from which they are being manifested. They are simply a phantasmagoria of Consciousness, and no matter how many worlds of desires, wishes, and positive and negative thoughts your mind creates, you should realize that they are all a play of Consciousness. When thoughts or images arise in your meditation, maintain the awareness of equality—the understanding that all objects are nothing but different forms of the Self. Be aware that even the worst thought is God. This understanding is vital to meditation. Your goal is not to battle with the mind, but to witness the mind. Know that you are the witness, the Self, and let the mind go wherever it likes. If you meditate with this awareness—that whatever is, is God—your mind will become calm very soon, and that will be high meditation.

Mantra

Another great means of dealing with the mind is to take the support of the mantra. In India there is a saying that the best way to take a thorn out of one's foot is with another thorn. In the same way, according to the scriptures, when one wants to still the mind, which revels in thoughts, one takes the help of one thought, the mantra.[23]

The word "mantra" means that which redeems and protects the one who contemplates it. Mantra is the very life of meditation, the greatest of all techniques. A mantra is a cosmic word or sound vibration. It is the vibration of the Self, the true speech of the Self, and, when we immerse ourselves in it, it leads us to the place of the Self.

Mantras consist of letters, which form words, which form sentences, which take us to their goal. Whether in mundane or spiritual life, all our work is carried out through mantras, through words. Without words, we cannot communicate with one another.

Mantras bear their fruit very quickly. The great saint Tukaram said, When the name of God is on the tongue, liberation is in your hand. This should not be surprising, because in mundane life we use words and they bear fruit immediately. I can make you happy immediately by using a few sweet words, by praising you and saying how beautiful you are. I can also make you agitated by using a few abusive words, by saying how bad you are.

Once a saint was giving a lecture on mantra. He was saying, "Mantra is great. Mantra takes us to God." Someone shouted from the back of the room, "How can you say that a mantra takes us to God? If I say, 'Bread, bread, bread,' will that get me bread?"

"Sit down, you bastard!" the saint shouted. When the man heard this, he became furious. He began to shake, and his hair stood on end. Even his necktie began to vibrate. He shouted, "You call yourself a saint, and yet you use such a filthy word for me?"

"I'm sorry, sir," the saint said. "Please, be calm and tell me what happened."

"You have the audacity to ask me what happened! Don't you realize how you have insulted me?"

"I used just one abusive word," the saint said, "and it has had such a powerful effect on you! When this is the case with an abusive term, what makes you think that the name of God, which is the supreme Truth, does not have its own power and will not also affect you?" If abusive words can make our blood boil, how can the name of God not have the power to change us?

Mantra has the greatest power. The sages of India, through the power of mantra, could burn whole mountains without fire. Through the power of mantra, they could bring entire universes into existence.

The scriptures say, *mantra Maheshvara*, mantra is God. There is no difference between God and His name; mantra has all the power of God. In the *Gita*, the Lord says: *mantro'ham*, [In all rituals] I am the mantra.[24] As we repeat the mantra, we should focus our attention within, on the place which is the source of the mantra. As we repeat the mantra more and more, it penetrates the entire territory of our mind, our intellect, and our imagination, and purifies it completely.

It is very important to repeat the mantra with the understanding of its meaning. Moreover, one who wants to attain the power of mantra, who wants to merge in mantra, should have the awareness that the goal of the mantra is one's own Self, that there is no difference between oneself, the mantra, and the goal of the mantra. If we hear an abusive word, we immediately identify ourselves as the object of that word, and that is why it has such an effect on us.

The only reason that a mantra does not affect us as profoundly as an abusive word is that we do not identify with it in the same way. If a person keeps himself, the mantra, and the goal of the mantra separate, he will never realize the goal of the mantra. Kashmir Shaivism says that we should meditate on God by becoming God; only then can we attain God.[25]

There are eighty-four million mantras that can be found in books or obtained from different teachers. However a mantra is not truly effective unless it is a conscious mantra, an alive mantra. A conscious mantra is one that has been received from a Guru who received it from his own Guru, repeated it himself, and attained full realization of his own inner Self. Such a mantra has the full power of the Guru's realization behind it, and when we repeat it in meditation, our meditation becomes infused with the force of that realization. The power that flows through such a Self-realized Guru is the grace-bestowing power of the Supreme, and that same power exists in his mantra. Traditionally, a Guru initiates a disciple through a mantra, and mantra is one of the means through which the Guru gives Shaktipat. As we repeat it with great love and reverence during meditation, it begins to work within. The energy of the Guru's conscious mantra, which is the energy of the supreme Guru, enters us and awakens our own inner energy, our own Shakti.

Asana

Another important factor in meditation is the sitting posture, or asana. The sitting posture is the foundation on which the whole structure of yoga rests. The *Yoga Sutras* say that the correct sitting posture is that in which one can sit comfortably for a long time.[26]

For meditation, the most important thing in asana is that the spine be kept straight. If the back is kept straight, the mind becomes steady in the heart.

There are three sitting postures which are suitable for meditation; however, if one is too uncomfortable sitting, one can stretch out on the back in *shavasana*, the corpse pose, and meditate in that position. The three main postures are *padmasana*, the lotus posture; *siddhasana*, the perfect posture; and *sukhasana*, the easy posture. Everyone must be familiar with the lotus posture, in which the legs are folded one over the other. The lotus is particularly important because, if one sits in this position for one and one-half hours, it will completely purify the 72,000 *nadis*, or inner subtle channels. If you cannot sit in the lotus posture, sit in the easy posture, with one leg folded over the other. If you keep sitting in either of these postures steadily, the mind will begin to turn inward, and meditation will happen on its own. When you keep moving the body continually, the mind becomes restless. As the posture becomes steady, the prana automatically becomes steady. As the prana becomes steady, the mind becomes steady, and, as the mind becomes steady, you begin to drink the joy that is in the heart.

Pranayama

The final factor in meditation is *pranayama*, the breathing process. People practice many different kinds of pranayama. Some people practice it so much that they ruin their minds, their intellects, and their bodies. In meditation the breathing process should be natural and spontaneous. We should not try to disturb the natural rhythm of the breath.

The mind and the prana work in conjunction with each other. So let the rhythm of your breathing be natural. As you repeat the mantra, the breath will go in and out in time with the rhythm of the mantra and will become steady by itself.

The Process of Meditation

There are four factors involved in meditation: the object of meditation, which is the inner Self; mantra, which is the vibration of the Self; asana, the posture in which we can sit comfortably for a long time; and natural pranayama, which arises when we repeat the mantra with love and reverence. These four factors are inter-related, and when they come together, meditation occurs in a very natural manner.

Meditation on the Self is very easy. All that we really need are love and interest. As we meditate more and more, the inner Shakti awakens and begins to unfold. The more intensely we long for medita-tion, the more we long for God, the more desire we have for the inner awakening, the closer we come to it. And the more we honor the Shakti, the more we revere and worship it, the more actively it works inside us. When three factors come together—our faith in the Shakti, the Shakti, and the Guru, who is the activator of the Shakti—there is an explosion of meditation within. Just as the Shakti creates universes in the outer world, when it begins to work inside us it creates a new inner universe, a universe of unend-ing enthusiasm, a universe of supreme bliss.

The inner universe is much greater than the outer universe; it is so vast that the entire outer cosmos can be kept in just one cor-ner of it. Everything is contained within it, and that is why, in meditation, the Indian seers were able to discover all the secrets of the universe.

Within us are infinite miracles, infinite wonders. As we go deeper into meditation, we come to understand the reality of all the dif-ferent inner worlds we read about in the scriptures. Within these inner spaces, nectarean music resounds—all the different musical instruments were originally made by yogis after they had listened to this inner music. Within us are such delicious nectars that noth-ing in this world can compare with them in sweetness. There are suns so effulgent that the outer sun looks dull beside them. We should meditate systematically and with great persistence and go deeper and deeper within the body. In this way, meditation will be a gradual unfolding of our inner being.

Along the way will be many experiences, and these experiences are fine. However the true state is beyond them. As we go deeper into meditation, we reach a place where we see nothing and hear nothing. Here there is nothing but bliss. This is the place of the Self, and true meditation is to become immersed in That.[27]

The seers of Vedanta explained that our spirit is encased not just in one body, but in four, and that as we meditate we pass through each of these four bodies to the Truth which lies within them.[28] The first is the physical body, in which we experience the waking state. This is the state in which we identify ourselves as the body. When we are in the waking state, if the body is experiencing pain and pleasure, we say, "I am experiencing pain," or "I am experiencing pleasure." As the Shakti begins to work in this body, we may experience physical movements, called *kriyas*, which are part of the process of purification of the physical body. In meditation, when the meditator is in the gross state, he can see the physical body as a red light which surrounds him like a flame of fire. This light is the size of the body, and within it one can see many marvelous things. Sometimes, one can even see the vital force and the different fluids circulating within the body.

As meditation deepens, the meditator passes from the gross body to the subtle body, which one can see as a white light. This light dwells in the throat center and is the size of the thumb. One experiences dreams in the subtle body; in this state one becomes aware that one is different from the physical body.

As the meditator goes deeper, he passes from the white, thumb-sized light to the light of the third body, which is black and the size of a fingertip. This is the causal body, the body of deep sleep. It is the state of total darkness, of total oblivion. In this state, the small self retires into the universal Self, and one is not even conscious of who or what one is. In this state, one experiences great peace. This is the state of the void.

However if a seeker has deep love for the Guru and has deep faith in his grace and in the Kundalini, he passes from the third plane to the fourth plane, the state of *turiya*, the transcendent state. Then, he sees the tiny blue light, the light of the Self, which we call the Blue Pearl.

The Blue Pearl is the most intimate body of the soul, and it is fascinatingly beautiful. As meditation deepens, one begins to see it sparkling and scintillating in the topmost spiritual center, the *sahasrara*. The Blue Pearl is the vehicle of the individual soul. It is in the Blue Pearl that the soul leaves the body after death and travels to different worlds. It is extremely fine and subtle, and it moves like lightning. Sometimes it comes out of the meditator's eyes and stands in front of him, moving so subtly that the eyes do not feel its passage.

The Blue Pearl is the size of a sesame seed, but in reality it is so vast that it contains the entire universe.[29] We are able to function because of the dynamism of the Blue Pearl. Because of its presence the breath moves in and out of our bodies. The rays of its divine love keep flowing through us, and because of these rays we feel love for each other. The light of the Blue Pearl lights up our faces and our hearts; it is because of this light that we give love to others. If this light left the body, the body would have no radiance and no attraction. It would be of no use to anyone, and it would have to be discarded. The Blue Pearl is the abode of God, the form of the Self within us. Once you begin to see it in yourself, you will also begin to see it in others. As you continue to meditate, one day this light will expand, and within it you will see the entire cosmos. As you become immersed in this light, you will know, "I am God. I am Brahman." It was after having this experience that the Sufi saint Mansur Mastana said, "Whatever I see around me is nothing but an expansion of my own being. I am not this body. I am the light which spreads everywhere."

This state is the culmination of meditation. In this state, our limitations vanish; our sense of individuality melts away. We attain divine vision, so that we no longer see this world as filled with duality and diversity. Instead of seeing differences between man and woman, East and West, past and future, we understand this whole universe as an expansion of our own Self. We realize that everything is a play of Consciousness and that, just as the bubbles and waves of the ocean arise and subside in the ocean, whatever exists arises and subsides in the Self.

It is to attain this state that one should meditate, that one's Shakti should be awakened. After one has reached this state, one no longer has to close one's eyes and sit for meditation; meditation goes on all the time. During formal meditation one experiences the highest bliss, but even in the waking state one experiences the joy of *samadhi*, seeing the entire waking world as an expansion of the same Consciousness. Wherever one looks, one sees God. Whatever one hears, one hears God. This is known as the state of natural samadhi, the state of the great beings, and in this state one continually drinks the bliss that is in the heart.

Siddha Meditation

If we are going to realize this state of oneness at the end of our practice of meditation, why should we not understand it at the beginning and practice meditation with the awareness that everything is Shiva? This is how the great beings meditate, and, if we also learn to see with this awareness, our meditation will be great. To meditate in this way we do not have to undergo any difficulties. We do not have to make the mind still. We do not even have to close our eyes. Utpaladeva, the great sage and philosopher of Kashmir Shaivism, says: *sarvo mamayam vibhava ityevam parijanatah;/Vishvatmano vikalpanam prasrepi maheshtah*, One who is constantly aware that this entire universe is his own glory retains his divinity even if thoughts and fancies play in his mind.[30]

Truly speaking, everything is Consciousness. It is only because of our sense of limited individuality that we see things differently. A man is Consciousness, a woman is Consciousness, a dog is Consciousness, a donkey is Consciousness, a stone is Consciousness, and a mountain is Consciousness. This is true understanding. This is the knowledge we obtain through meditation, and the moment we obtain this knowledge we begin to understand everything as it is.

In order to rid yourself of the feeling of limitation and obtain this understanding, you should practice the sadhana of Shiva. You should understand, "I am Shiva—God. It is God who is meditating, and all the objects of my meditation are God. My sadhana is God, and everybody and everything I see is God." For a long time you have had the awareness, "I am an individual being; I am small; I am limited." This is why it is difficult for you to accept immediately the awareness, "I am God." All your life you have been hearing that you are a sinner. Your teachers, all the holy books, and people pursuing different religious paths have been telling you that you are a sinner, and you have come to believe it. In this way you impose the idea of sin onto the Self, which is totally pure and free of sin. It is because one has this wrong understanding that one identifies oneself with the wrong things. That is why one cannot uplift oneself; that is why one cannot have faith in the Self or become one-pointed on the Self. Kashmir Shaivism teaches that when one begins to think, "I am this, I am that, I am a sinner, I am an inferior person," one becomes poor in Shakti, and that is how one becomes an individual being.

In Vedanta, this is often explained by a story. One day, a washerman took several donkeys to a forest to graze them. There, he came upon a lion cub; he did not know that it was a lion, and he brought it home with him. The lion cub grew up with the donkeys. Living in their company, he began to repeat the donkey mantra, Hee-haw, hee-haw, to eat with them, and to travel back and forth to the river carrying filthy laundry. As the lion grew up, he thought of himself as a donkey and shared the donkeys' habits and their ways.

One day when he was grazing on the river bank with his donkey brothers, another lion came along to drink from the river. While this lion was drinking, he suddenly caught sight of the young lion in the midst of the donkeys. The old lion was shocked to see his brother in such a pitiful condition. He moved closer to him and said, "Brother, what are you up to?"

"I am with my brothers," said the young lion.

"How can you call them brothers? They are asses and you are a lion. Come with me and look at your reflection in the water. Look at your reflection and my reflection, and see if there is anything similar about us."

The young lion gazed down at his reflection and saw that he looked just like the old lion.

"Are they your brothers or am I your brother? Now stop going Hee-haw and start roaring!"

The young lion began to roar, and all the donkeys ran away. The two lions ran into the forest. The young lion had been transformed from a donkey to a lion; he had become free.

Actually, the lion cub had never been a donkey. He had only thought he was a donkey, and this is exactly the situation we are in. We are not donkeys. We are not limited, imperfect beings. We are not sinners. We never became small; we only believe we are small. So we must discard this belief and become aware of our own strength. Kashmir Shaivism says that when Chiti, universal Consciousness, accepts limitations, it begins to believe itself to be bound.[31] Just as Chiti becomes smaller and smaller by descending from its status as pure Consciousness and becomes a limited individual soul, when it reverses the process it can become greater and greater and regain its original nature. It is only our awareness which has to be changed. We never became donkeys, and we never can become donkeys, because we are the pure Self.

To rid yourself of wrong understanding you do not have to do anything new. All you have to do is meditate. The fact is that you meditate not to attain God, but to become aware that God is within you. Kashmir Shaivism says: *nashivam vidyate kvachit,* Nothing

exists which is not Shiva.[32] Where is that place where there is no
Shiva? Where is that time where there is no Shiva? So even if you
experience duality, even if you see diversity around you, consider
yourself to be Shiva. Understand that it is Shiva who is eating, Shiva
who is the food that is eaten, Shiva who gives, and Shiva who takes.
It is Shiva who does everything. The entire universe is the glory of
Shiva, the glory of the Self.

Meditation Instructions

PREPARING FOR MEDITATION

It is very good to set aside a place for meditation. If possible,
have a special room, but if not, a corner will do. Purify it by chanting God's name, and try not to let anything take place there which
will disturb its atmosphere. In the place where you meditate regularly, the vibrations of meditation gather, and after a while it
becomes very easy to meditate there. For the same reason, you
should set aside special clothes and a mat for meditation; do not
wash them too often, because the Shakti will accumulate in them
and make it easy for you to meditate.

If possible, meditate at the same time every day. The early
hours of the morning, between 3:00 A.M. and 6:00 A.M., are the best
for meditation, but you can meditate at any time which is conve-
nient. If you become accustomed to meditating at a certain hour
your body will develop the habit of meditation. I have been meditating every morning at three o'clock for many years, and even now
my body automatically goes into meditation at that hour.

THE ATTITUDE OF MEDITATION

Just as you slip easily into sleep, you should be able to slip easily into meditation. Sit peacefully; be with yourself. Focus your mind
on the inner Consciousness, the inner knower. Let your breath move
naturally and watch it; do not force anything. Become immersed in

your own inner Self. Turn your mind and senses inward. Absorb yourself in the pure "I."

If thoughts arise, let them come and go. Watch the source of your thoughts. Meditate with the awareness that you are the witness of the mind. True meditation is to become free from mentation. The moment the thoughts become still, the light of the Self will shine from within. However if the mind does not immediately become thought-free, do not try to erase the thoughts forcibly. Respect the mind, understanding that whatever comes and goes within it is a form of the Self. Then it will become still on its own.

To help in stilling the mind, you may take the support of the mantra. Repeat either *Om Namah Shivaya* or *So'ham.* Both mantras are one; both come from the Self. Only the method of repeating them differs.

OM NAMAH SHIVAYA

Om Namah Shivaya means, I bow to the Lord, who is the inner Self. Repeat it silently, at the same rate of speed with which you speak. Repeat it with love, and go deep inside. Understand that you yourself are the deity of the mantra. Listen to it. When every letter pulsates in your mind, try to experience it.

Lose yourself in meditation. No matter what feeling arises, let it be. Do not fear. The inner energy is filled with infinite techniques, processes, and feelings. Its play is in everything. Therefore, everything belongs to it, and it is one with your Self.

The purpose of meditation is inner happiness, inner peace. It is fine to have visions, but they are not absolutely necessary. What is necessary is inner joy. When all the senses become quiet and you experience bliss, that is the attainment. The world is the embodiment of joy; joy lies everywhere. Find it and attain it. Instead of having negative thoughts, have the awareness, "I am pure; I am joy." Feel good about yourself; fill yourself with great divinity.

Meditate with this understanding: "Neither am I different from God, nor is God different from me." Then, not only will you attain God, but you yourself will become God.

Become quiet with the awareness that everything is you and you are everything.

Meditate on your Self. Honor your Self. Understand your Self. God dwells within you as you.

Your own,

रव्यामे मुक्तानंद.

Swami Muktananda

LOOKING WITHIN
Gurumayi Chidvilasananda

Swami Muktananda always said, "You can attain the Truth instantly when you receive grace." Often we feel we have to meditate for a long, long time in order to experience the Truth. But this is just an idea we have. If you really want it, a second is enough. Every second of your life contains the power of meditation; every second contains both the power of the Truth and the power to experience it.

What is meditation? It has been described by many different people in many ways. Everyone has his own experience. Long ago, the sages began to wonder: "What is this power which makes everything move and which also makes everything still? What is this power?" They discussed it, they argued about it, they speculated and conjectured very intelligently, at great length, but nothing worked. They simply could not come to any conclusion. After days and weeks and months and years, one day, spontaneously, they found themselves in deep meditation. They found themselves within themselves. They said:

Those who are devoted to meditation and contemplation
See the divine energy hidden in its own qualities.
It is the One who rules over all causes from time to the soul.[33]

This was their experience. When they went deep inside themselves, in meditation, they experienced the power within. The same divine energy exists within everyone. When you go inside, it is awakened. If you only wander around the world outside, you do not experience the awakened energy that lives within you. You simply stay on the surface of life and you feel you're not in touch with yourself. No matter what is happening, you feel lost. The sages found themselves in meditation.

In the words of Swami Muktananda, "Meditation is looking within." This does not mean just sitting with your eyes closed, even though this is the first step of meditation. It means performing all your actions—when you talk, as you live—and looking within at the same time. When there is no looking within, you lose touch with your own divine energy and there is no true joy.

"Those who are devoted to meditation and contemplation see the divine energy hidden in its own qualities." Everything contains this incredible power, this force. When you experience it, you see light everywhere, you find joy in everything. You experience happiness in times of happiness, but you are also able to experience happiness in the midst of sorrow. This is the greatness of meditation.

As you look within, you have the experience of your own inner Self. As long as you don't know who you really are, the Truth escapes you. You find the Truth when you come to know your own inner Self. Then, it is always there, always with you.

Once there was a man named John McCormick who lived in Glasgow. Night after night, he kept having the same dream, in which a mysterious voice whispered in his ear, "London Bridge... under London Bridge lies a great treasure. It's yours, go find it..." Every morning John McCormick woke up smiling, but he did not take the dream seriously. John McCormick was a poor man. He needed money all the time. So, naturally, he assumed he had imagined, literally dreamt up a fortune. Nevertheless, night after night, night after night, the same dream, the same voice: "Under London Bridge... under London Bridge... it's yours... treasure..."

Finally, one day, John McCormick decided he had to set out for London. It was a long, painful journey for a man with little money. But after many weeks he did arrive at London Bridge. And there, much to his astonishment, he found the Queen's guards posted at both ends of the bridge. He could not think of a way to dig up the treasure without the guards seeing him. In his bafflement, he began to walk up and down, up and down. He took a room in a little inn nearby and every day he went to the bridge and tried to figure out where the treasure was buried, and how to get it.

One of the officers watched this fellow appear every day, and walk up and down. Finally, he decided to speak to him. "What are you doing here? Are you waiting for somebody, or have you lost something?"

John McCormick hesitated. He took a long look at the officer's face. He seemed to be a very sympathetic, kind man. So John McCormick decided to open his heart to this stranger and told him about his dream.

When he heard the story, the officer began to laugh. "You listened to a dream? I don't believe it! You wore out your shoes, spent your money and your strength to come all the way here—for a dream? If I were to do such a foolish thing—follow a dream—do you know where I would be right now?"

With that, the officer began to relate a dream that kept recurring to him. "I have been having the same dream for months," he said. "A mysterious voice keeps whispering, 'Go to Glasgow... to the house of John McCormick. There, in a dirty corner, behind the stove, lies a great treasure...'" The officer laughed at himself. "Now, I ask you, Sir, how would a soldier like me get to Glasgow? And even if I did, half the men in Scotland are named John and the other half, McCormick. And suppose I found one of them and started tearing up the floor of his house—what do you suppose they would do to me?"

John McCormick listened to the officer's dream very seriously. In his heart, he bowed deeply to the Lord. Then without another word he left London Bridge and returned home—straight to the dirty corner behind the stove. He took a shovel, he dug up the earth—and he found the treasure that lay buried in his own house.

This is the story of everyone's life. You look everywhere. You perform many spiritual practices. You go high into the mountains and meditate for many many years. Sometimes, nothing happens and you come home dejected. "Why did I go there?" The moment you say that, an experience suddenly explodes inside you. You realize the high mountain lies within you. The spiritual quality of that mountain *is* you. This is what happened to all the sages of the Vedas, to all the great beings and meditators. Discussion got them nowhere. But when they closed their eyes and looked within, they found treasure, God's treasure, the incredible experience.

> *In this vast wheel of creation*
> *Which gives life to all things,*
> *In which everything rests,*
> *The soul flutters about,*
> *Thinking that its own Self and God are different.*
> *Then, when blessed by God*
> *One gains eternal life.*[34]

Our fear is created out of this disparity, "God and I are different." When we have this feeling about God, we feel the same way about the world. "People and I are different. Things and I are different." This duality provokes so much fear, because it places everybody, including God, far away and separate from us. When there is such distance between God and us, "the soul flutters." There is such fear, we tremble. Our thoughts frighten us. Our actions frighten us. Having to go somewhere frightens us. There is no rest whatsoever, there is no peace—only restlessness, continuous restlessness.

So the sages say, "Look within. Meditate. You will find Oneness. You will discover there is no difference between you and God. God is within you." As long as we do not have this experience, we cannot be at peace with ourselves.

Everyone is always talking about world peace. When we hold public programs, all sorts of people come. Afterward, many of them come up in the *darshan* line and say, "There should be peace in the world. There must be world peace." You open a magazine and it also says there should be peace in the world. You open a brochure, you talk to a friend—everybody's saying there should be peace in the world. Where is the world? Where is it? It's you and I. If there is no peace within you, how can there be peace in the world? We must experience peace within ourselves. It is not as if someone in the world is going to click suddenly and produce peace. It is not as if somebody can push a button on a computer and program peace on earth. It has to happen inside each of us. However difficult this may seem, peace does occur. Look within: meditation happens. Then you discover peace, your own peace, within you.

There was a great samurai once who did not believe in anything spiritual. However, people kept talking to him about God. So, one day, reluctantly, he visited a great saint. He asked him, "Is there such a thing as heaven? Is there such a place as hell?"

The saint looked up and said, "Beggar! Who would want to talk about such things with the likes of you!"

The samurai was outraged. He drew his sword. But the saint only smiled and said, "So, the beggar has a sword."

The samurai had so much pride, he was beside himself. He raised his sword in fury and was about to strike the saint, when the old man spoke again, very softly and gently, without even looking up: "There open the gates of hell."

When the samurai heard this, his whole body trembled. He knelt and laid his sword down. His head hung low and tears started rolling down his cheeks. In a soft voice, the saint said, "Here open the gates of heaven."

Where is heaven? Where is hell? Within us. Each one can create a heaven, each one can create a hell. People ask, "Does a human being have free will, or does everything happen because of destiny?" The crux of the matter is, a human being does have so much power. Each one creates his own destiny out of his own free will. Look within. Meditate. It just happens. You find your own joy, you find your own peace.

The sages said:

> Matter is perishable.
> God is imperishable and immortal.
> The one God rules over both the perishable and the soul.
> By meditating on Him, by uniting with Him,
> By reflecting more and more on His being,
> The illusion of the world comes to an end.[35]

We reflect on many things. We feel we are very complicated, but the sages say, when we reflect on God, on the being of God, the illusion of the world comes to an end. You feel free. You experience your own serenity and your own greatness.

Once, it is said, three great beings came together and began exchanging views on the nature of the world. As they spoke, an angel appeared. She held a golden cup in her hand. "Drink this," she said. "This is the nectar of the world. It will tell you what the world is like."

So, one of them took a sip, held it in his mouth awhile, and then swallowed it. "How is it?" asked the others.

"So-so," he replied. "Could be good, could be bad."

The second one took a sip and immediately an expression of distaste came over his face. "Horrible. Disgusting. I would never want to live in the world." And he, too, passed the cup of the world.

The third great being took one small sip, and then another—and then he drained the goblet dry. The other two were astonished and asked, "Does the world taste good to you?"

"The world has no taste of its own," he answered. "Whatever you add to it, that's what it tastes like. You furnish your own flavor and then the world appears that way to you. The world itself is free from everything."

"Matter is perishable," say the Upanishads. "God is imperishable and immortal." Look within. Meditate. Savor the peace that lies within you. As we reflect on our own inner Self, that which is not necessary falls away. Only the kernel of the experience remains with us.

The act of contemplation awakens grace. When you put forth the right kind of effort in contemplation, in reflection, you experience grace permeating your entire being. Then you don't have to be afraid of what you may say. Whatever you say is because of grace. Your speaking, your hearing, your sight are all because of grace.

Once, a great saint named Rabi'a saw a man walking down the road with a bandage around his forehead, groaning. She asked him what was wrong.

"I have a terrible, terrible headache," he answered. "I don't know what to do to cure it."

"How long have you had it?" she asked.

"Two days."

"How old are you?"

"Thirty years old."

"Has this ever happened to you before?"

"No, this is the first time in my life," the young man said. "That's why it's so upsetting."

"Oh," Rabi'a said. "You've never had a headache. For thirty years, you did not have one. Now you have a headache for only two days and you go around showing off the pain. You are wearing a bandage of ungratefulness. Tell me, all these years, have you ever worn a bandage of gratitude?"

Reflect on this. We forget our good days and we remember our bad days. This is why we feel nothing works—because our way of thinking is not always right. In the beginning, the practice of contemplation is soul-searching. You go through one tunnel after the other, you go through one pain after the other, one joy after the other. And sometimes, this reflection can become unbearable because you see yourself. Your whole life is presented before your eyes. Nevertheless, this reflection, this act of contemplation removes all that which is unnecessary. You're left lighthearted with only one thing: the experience of grace, the experience of Shakti, divine energy.

> *When fire is latent in wood, it cannot be seen*
> *Yet its seed is not destroyed.*
> *It can be made to manifest again and again by friction.*
> *Similarly, the inner Self must be made to manifest in the body*
> *By means of the syllable Om.*[36]

Again and again, we chant the mantra O*m*, the inner sound. Repeating it creates a friction, and out of this friction is created fire, the fire of grace. It awakens the inner energy and you see your own inner Self in its light. This seeing is not just an image. It is the absolute Reality. It is not just an idea. It is the Truth. "When fire is latent in wood, it cannot be seen, yet its seed is not destroyed." Therefore it is said, let whatever you do be an offering to God. Whatever action you perform, offer it to God. Then, because you have not attached strings to it, it is free from selfishness. Because of this, the fruits you attain from your actions become greater.

Once a seeker went to a great saint and begged him for an experience of the Truth. The sage invited him to stay overnight. Evening was falling. The sage rose and the seeker's heart began to beat with expectation. But, without a word, the sage began to light seventy candles.

"Wait a minute," the seeker protested. "I didn't come here to perform rituals and ceremonies. I don't want anything to do with these outer displays. I want to experience God within me. Give me That."

Undisturbed, the saint completed his act of worship. Then he turned to the seeker and said, "You can put out the candles if you want. Understand, I have lighted each one for God. If there is any candle I have not lit for him, go ahead and put it out."

With that, he retired to his room and the seeker began *his* ritual, trying to extinguish the flames. But nothing would go out. Not a single flame. And there were seventy candles! He poured water on them, he poured sand on them. He used his mighty breath to blow them out. All night long, he persisted but, in the morning, when the saint woke up, seventy flames still burned.

"Did you change your mind?" said the sage.

"No, I tried," said the seeker. "But I couldn't put them out."

The sage said, "I told you I lit every flame for God. This was not an empty ritual. It was an expression of gratitude. Gratitude can never be extinguished."

In the same way, every action you perform should be a candle lighted for God. Then, nobody can erase it—not your own ego or anyone else's. Only then will you find true joy. We should perform every action for God, not in name only but with our entire being—in our waking state, in our dream state, in our deep-sleep state—in every state of consciousness. Not just mentally or intellectually, not just with the heart, either, but with our entire being, we should offer our actions. Let even the experience of peace be for God, for the experience of God within.

In the same way, offer your inhalation to your exhalation and your exhalation to your inhalation. It is a very simple offering: your own breath. It is yours and yet it is not yours. When you do this, you find yourself gliding into meditation easily. When you do not make this offering, you remain on the surface of the mind caught in the web of its thoughts and images and ideas and fantasies. If you go to the source of the mind, you are with God. Offer your inhalation to your exhalation, your exhalation to your inhalation. As you reflect on this, you know it is one breath.

What supports this breath? The heart inside or the heart outside? The space within or the space without? What supports this breath, which goes in and comes out so freely? It is a great miracle. This breath fans the fire of life. So as you make this offering, you experience exhilaration and incredible serenity at the same time. As the breath becomes calmer, the mind becomes calmer. As the mind becomes calmer, the breath becomes calmer. As your entire being becomes calm, it is no effort to look within. Meditation is just happening.

> Just as a mirror covered with dust shines brightly
> When it has been cleaned,
> Once a person has seen the true nature of the Self,
>   the inner Self,
> He becomes integrated, fulfilled, and free from sorrow.[37]

In the days of the Vedas, a powerful king invited a great spiritual Master to his palace and asked him for initiation. "The next time I come here, I will do it," the great Master told him. But the second time he came he said, "First, I must have my meal and then I will initiate you into the Truth."

The king was delighted and led the sage to a table set with golden dishes.

"I don't want to eat from your golden plate, I want to eat from my own bowl," the sage said, drawing a monk's simple begging bowl from his robes. "Please, put the food in this."

The king took the bowl gladly, but when he went to put food in it, he saw that it was very dirty. Even a less fastidious host would not want to put his delicious food in such a dirty bowl. So, the king went to clean it himself. But the stains were so deeply embedded, they would not wash away, no matter how hard the king scrubbed. In the end, he returned the bowl to the Master, saying, "Your bowl is very dirty. Please let me get you a clean plate, fit for good clean food."

The great Master began to laugh. "O King, this bowl is not a part of me, and yet you don't want to sully your food with it. What makes you think I can put the purest teachings into the dirty bowl that is inside you? Clean that first. Then I will not even have to initiate you. The experience will just happen."

This cleansing takes place through truthfulness and austerity, two beautiful words, which are a part of every path. "Austerity" does not mean staying up all night or eating roots and berries, wearing clothes made from the bark of trees or sleeping on a bed of nails. There is no austerity greater than overcoming the trouble of your own mind. This form of austerity is very simple: it is looking within. The moment you take a look at yourself, grace is in your glance, grace is in your vision. All that is unnecessary melts away. The fire in your vision burns away the impressions in your being.

Whenever someone asked Baba for his grace, Baba said, "There must be disciple's grace first." The grace of the disciple is very important. When you look within, you bestow your grace upon yourself. Again and again, no matter where you go, the same path is shown: turn within, look within. Then you understand the meaning of the scripture:

Om *purnamadah purnamidam*
Purnat *purnamudacyate*
Purnasya *purnamadaya*
Purnamevavasishyate

That is perfect, this is perfect.
From the perfect springs the perfect.
If from the perfect, the perfect be taken,
Only the perfect remains.

This perfection is inner grace. In this perfection you find complete repose. When stillness courses through your every action, you are with God. Then God is not some entity which is far away, not something created by the mind, but a true experience. Then your action is like the flame of the candle lit by the saint. It is for God and it is forever. It is for this experience that we meditate.

Sadgurunath Maharaj ki Jay!

SIDDHA MEDITATION
In Our Daily Life

The awakening of our inner Shakti by the Guru is the greatest gift we can receive. We learn to nurture this energy so that it can unfold and bestow its many blessings within us. A disciplined life is a great support to our meditation practice, and the natural intoxication of the meditative state will, in turn, help to loosen the binding knots of any negative behavior patterns in our lives.

Here are some practical guidelines for the pursuit of Siddha Meditation.

Crucial to setting up a meditation practice is the commitment to meditate, however briefly, every day. One particularly powerful time for meditation is the predawn hours of 3 to 6 A.M., known as *Brahmamuhurta*, when the mind is irresistibly drawn inside. However, any time of day is fine. It is helpful to meditate at the same time each day, to set aside a special meditation room or corner in your house, and to reserve a woolen blanket or mat to sit on. This invites the mind to return to the inner realms naturally and easily.

To accustom oneself to meditation, it is good to begin by sitting for fifteen to twenty minutes. Allow this to increase bit by bit. When you feel ready you can meditate for an hour at a time.

JAPA

Silent repetition of the mantra is known as japa. As we repeat the mantra, Om Namah Shivaya, our minds become pure and light. The mantra can be mingled with the breath, repeated silently once with each inhalation and with each exhalation, or it may take its own rhythm within. It can be repeated any time the mind is free: in the midst of activity or when lying down to sleep at night. With each repetition the energy of the mantra builds inside, vitalizing us and giving us access to deeper experiences.

CHANTING

Chanting releases the fountain of joy in the heart. It stills the mind and prepares it for meditation. Chanting can be a group or solitary activity. It purifies the very atmosphere of the place where it is done: for this reason many people like to chant or play tapes of chanting in their homes.

STUDY

It is good to begin or end your day by contemplating the Truth. Reading the Master's words on a regular basis helps us to understand the path of Siddha Yoga as well as our own experiences on the path.

SATSANG

Satsang means keeping the company of the Truth, sharing with other people in a way that touches upon and brings out what is most profound in us. It also refers to keeping the company of our own genuine aspirations. Gathering together with others to experience the spiritual path can be very beneficial. There are Siddha Yoga centers and ashrams where programs of chanting and meditation are held regularly. For information about centers, call SYDA Foundation Centers Office.

DARSHAN

Darshan means to directly perceive the Truth, or embodiment of the Truth, a saint. Spending time in the company of the Guru is the most powerful satsang of all. Gurumayi Chidvilasananda travels frequently, giving programs and Intensives all over the world. For Gurumayi's schedule, write or call SYDA Foundation.

THE INTENSIVE

The Intensive is the single most important program offered in Siddha Yoga. In the Intensive, divine initiation, known as Shaktipat, is bestowed by Gurumayi Chidvilasananda. Through Shaktipat, the Guru's own spiritual energy awakens the great force called Kundalini, which lies dormant in every human being, and meditation occurs easily and spontaneously. Taking the Intensive is one of the most effective spiritual practices we can perform.

SIDDHA
MEDITATION
Ashrams and Centers

Siddha Meditation is practiced in more than 600 ashrams and centers around the world. For information regarding the one nearest you, contact:

GURUDEV SIDDHA PEETH
P.O. Ganeshpuri (PIN 401-206)
District Thana, Maharashtra
India

CENTERS OFFICE
SYDA FOUNDATION
P.O. Box 600
South Fallsburg, NY 12779
(914) 434-2000

NOTES

1. *Bhagavad Gita*, chap. 13, v. 1.

2. Ibid., chap. 13, v. 2.

3. Shankaracharya, *Atmabodha*, v. 36.

4. See *Chandogya Upanishad*, book 7, chap. 6, v. l.

5. See Shankaracharya, *Atmabodha*, v. 22: "Attachment, desire, pleasure, pain are perceived to exist only as long as the mind functions... Therefore, they belong to the mind alone and not to the Self."

6. *Brihajjabala Upanishad*, book 8, v. 6.

7. Kshemaraja, *Pratyabhijnahridayam*, sutra. 1.

8. For further information about Kundalini, see Swami Muktananda, *Kundalini: The Secret of Life*, and *Play of Consciousness*.

9. Knowledge refers here to the direct perceptual experience in which the Self is "seen" illuminating itself, without the aid of the senses, mind, or intellect.

10. See *Vijnana Bhairava*, v. 98: *ichhayam athava jnane jate chittam niveshayet/atmabuddhyananyachetas tatas tattvarthadarshanam*, "When a desire, or knowledge, or activity appears, one should, with the mind withdrawn from all objects [of desire, knowledge, etc.], fix the mind on that desire,…understanding it as the Self. Then, one will have the realization of the essential Reality."

11. *Yoga Vasishtha*.

12. Shiva, in this connection, refers not to the Hindu deity, but to the all-pervasive Consciousness, or God, of which Shiva is one name.

13. See Abhinavagupta, *Tantrasara*, "The net of sadhana cannot reveal Shiva. Can a clay pot illuminate the conscious sun?"

14. Although the Self is self-luminous and does not depend on any outside agency to be experienced, the intellect, mind, and other instruments serve as vehicles through which the Self is approached. Therefore, Self-realization cannot take place unless they are refined and purified.

15. See Patanjali, *Yoga Sutras*, book 1, sutra 2: *yogash chitta vritti nirodhaha*, "Yoga is to still the ripples of the mind"; and sutra 3, *tada drashtuh svarupe vasthanam*, "Then the seer is established in his own essential nature."

16. Patanjali, *Yoga Sutras*, book 3, sutra 1.

17. *Brihadaranyaka* Upanishad, chap. 3, sec. 7, v. 20.

18. *Kena Upanishad*, chap. 1, v. 5.

19. *Bhagavad Gita*, chap. 13, v. 14.

20. *Mundaka Upanishad*, chap. 2, sec. 1, v. 3: "From Him are born life, mind, all the sense organs..."

21. Kshemaraja, *Pratyabhijnahridayam*, sutra 5.

22. Ibid., sutra 2.

23. See Patanjali, *Yoga Sutras*, book 1, sutras 27-29. According to Vyasa, an early commentator on the *Yoga Sutras*, "The repetition of mantra and contemplation of its goal allow the mind to become concentrated."

24. *Bhagavad Gita*, chap. 9, v. 16.

25. See Somananda, Shiva Drishti: *shivo'smi sadhanavishtaha shivo'ham yajako'pyaham/shivam yami shivo yami shivena shiva sadhanaha,* "Practice sadhana with the following awareness: I am a form of Shiva. I will attain Shiva. By becoming Him, I will attain Him. Because I am Shiva, I will attain Shivahood very easily. This is the sadhana to attain Shiva."

26. Patanjali, *Yoga Sutras,* book 2, sutra 46.

27. In this state, the mind and senses are stilled, yet there is total awareness. See Swami Muktananda, *Play of Consciousness,* chap. 24.

28. For a more detailed description of meditation in the four bodies, see Swami Muktananda, *Play of Consciousness.*

29. Tukaram Maharaj, the seventeenth-century Maharashtrian poet-saint, says in one of his verses: "God, the nourisher of the universe, has made his dwelling place in a house as small as a sesame seed."

30. Utpaladeva, *Ishvara Pratyabhijna,* sec. 4, chap. 1, v. 12.

31. Kshemaraja, *Pratyabhijnahridayam,* sutra 9: *chidvat tacchakti sankochat malavritaha samsari,* "Because of contraction, universal Consciousness becomes an ordinary being, subject to limitations."

32. *Svacchanda Tantra.* Quoted by Swami Muktananda, *Siddha Meditation,* p. 74.

33. *Shvetashvatara Upanishad,* I, 3

34. *Shvetashvatara Upanishad,* I, 6

35. *Shvetashvatara Upanishad,* I, 10

36. *Shvetashvatara Upanishad,* I, 13

37. *Shvetashvatara Upanishad,* II, 14

GLOSSARY

Absolute: The highest Reality; supreme Consciousness; the pure, untainted, changeless Truth.

Aham: (lit. "I") The pure inner Self; absolute I; the experiencing subject; "I"-consciousness.

Aham Brahmasmi: One of the four mahavakyas, or great statements, of Vedanta. It means "I am Brahman," the supreme Absolute. *See also* Vedanta.

Apana: Inhalation; one of the five types of prana; the downward moving energy that controls the abdomen and excretion of wastes from the body. *See also* Prana.

Arjuna: One of the warrior heroes from the *Mahabharata* epic; a great disciple of Lord Krishna. It was to Arjuna that Krishna imparted his teachings in the *Bhagavad Gita*.

Asana: 1) A hatha yoga posture practiced to strengthen the body, purify the nervous system, and develop one-pointedness of mind; the yoga texts refer to eighty-four major asanas. 2) A seat or mat on which one sits for meditation.

Ashram: A community where spiritual discipline is practiced; the abode of a saint or holy person.

Austerity: 1) Rigorous spiritual practice. 2) Abandonment of the pursuit of worldly pleasure for the purpose of spiritual attainment.

Ayurvedic Medicine: The ancient Indian science of health, still widely practiced, which is based on the Vedic scriptures. It teaches that good health depends on maintaining an even balance of the elements in the body.

Bayazid Bistami, Hazrit or *Abu Yazid al-Bestami*: (d. circa 875) Born in Bestam in northeastern Persia, where his tomb stands today, he was a Sufi saint of the Naqshbandi Order and the author of many poems, which boldly portray the mystic's total absorption in God.

Bhagavad Gita: (lit. "The Song of the Lord") One of the world's greatest works of spiritual literature, part of the epic the *Mahabharata*. In the *Gita*, Lord Krishna explains the path of liberation to Arjuna on the battlefield. *See also* Arjuna; Krishna.

Bhagawan: (lit. "the Lord") One who is glorious, illustrious, and venerable. A term of great honor. Baba Muktananda's Guru is known as Bhagawan Nityananda. *See also* Nityananda, Bhagawan.

Blue Pearl (nila bindu): A brilliant blue light, the size of a tiny seed, which appears to the meditator whose energy has been awakened. The bindu is the subtle abode of the inner Self.

Brahman: Vedantic term for the Absolute Reality.

Brihajjabala Upanishad: One of the minor Upanishads, from the *Atharva Veda*. *See also* Upanishads; Vedas.

Chakra: (lit. "wheel") An energy center located in the subtle body. There are seven major chakras. When the Kundalini is awakened, it flows upward from the muladhara chakra at the base of the spine to the sahasrara at the crown of the head. *See also* Kundalini.

Chidvilasananda, Swami: (*Chidvilasananda*, lit. "the bliss of the play of Consciousness") The name given to Gurumayi by her Guru, Baba Muktananda, in 1982, when she took the vows of monkhood.

Chiti: Divine conscious energy; the creative aspect of God. *See also* Kundalini; Shakti.

Consciousness: The intelligent, supremely independent, divine energy which creates, pervades, and supports the entire universe. *See also* Chiti; Shakti.

Contemplation: The process of reflecting on the significance of one's existence. Contemplation strips away the layers of illusion, bringing one closer to the experience of the Self within.

Darshan line: The line which is formed as people come forward to pay their respects to the Guru.

Dharana: 1) Concentration; the sixth of the eight limbs of the path of raja yoga. In this limb (phase of practice), the mind becomes stabilized by being fixed on an object. 2) A centering technique described in the *Vijnana Bhairava*. *See also* Patanjali; *Yoga Sutras*; *Vijnana Bhairava*.

Disciple: One who has received initiation from a Master and then follows the path shown by the Master with great enthusiasm and commitment. *See also* Guru; Practices; Shaktipat.

Disciple's grace: An attitude of longing, surrender, acceptance, gratitude, faith, and devotion in the disciple's relationship to the Guru, which allows the disciple to receive fully the fruits of spiritual practice.

Ego: The limited sense of "I" identified with the body, mind, and senses; sometimes described as the veil of suffering.

Enlightenment: The final attainment on the spiritual path, when the limited sense of "I" merges into supreme Consciousness. *See also* Liberation; Self-realization.

Ganeshpuri: A village at the foot of Mandagni Mountain in Maharashtra, India. Bhagawan Nityananda settled in this region, where yogis have performed spiritual practices for thousands of years. Gurudev Siddha Peeth, the ashram founded by Baba Muktananda at his Guru's command, is built on this sacred land. The samadhi shrines of Bhagawan Nityananda and of Swami Muktananda, located here, attract many thousands of pilgrims every year.

Gita: (lit. "song") See also *Bhagavad Gita; Guru Gita.*

Grace: The infinite power of divine love that creates, maintains, and pervades the universe. When awakened within a seeker by a Siddha Guru, this power leads the seeker to Self-realization. *See also* Self-realization; Shaktipat.

Guru: (lit. "from darkness to light") A spiritual teacher or Master who has attained oneness with God. A true Guru initiates seekers into the spiritual path and guides them to liberation. *See also* Shaktipat.

Guru Gita: (lit. "song of the Guru") An ancient Sanskrit text which describes the nature of the Guru, the Guru-disciple relationship, and meditation on the Guru. In Siddha Yoga ashrams the *Guru Gita* is chanted every morning. *See also* Guru.

Gurudev Siddha Peeth: (*Siddha Peeth*, lit. "abode of a Siddha") The main ashram of Gurumayi and of Siddha Yoga, and the site of the samadhi shrine of Baba Muktananda. Founded in 1956, when Bhagawan Nityananda instructed Muktananda to live in a simple three-room compound near Ganeshpuri, India, it is now a world-renowned spiritual center. *See also* Ashram; Ganeshpuri.

Gurumayi: (lit. "one who is absorbed in the Guru") A Marathi term of respect used in addressing Swami Chidvilasananda.

Hatha Yoga: Yogic practices, both physical and mental, done for the purpose of purifying the physical and subtle bodies. The goal of hatha yoga is to awaken the inner energy, or Kundalini.

Initiation: See Shaktipat.

Kashmir Shaivism: A nondual philosophy that recognizes the entire universe as a manifestation of Chiti, the divine conscious energy. This Shaivite philosophical tradition explains how the formless supreme Principle, Shiva, manifests as the universe. Together with Vedanta, Kashmir Shaivism provides the basic scriptural context for Siddha Yoga. *See also Shiva Sutras.*

Kena Upanishad: (*Kena*, lit. "by whom") A principal Upanishad, which establishes that Brahman is the supreme Reality by whom the mind, speech, and senses perform their functions. *See also* Upanishads.

Krishna: (lit. "the dark one," "the one who attracts irresistibly") The eighth incarnation of Vishnu. Lord Krishna's life story is described in the *Shrimad Bhagavatam* and the *Mahabharata*, and his spiritual teachings are contained in the *Bhagavad Gita.*

Kriya Yoga: The yoga whereby the individual utilizes his senses, breath, and mind for Self-realization.

Kriyas: (lit. "movements") Purificatory movements—physical, mental, and emotional—initiated by the awakened Kundalini. *See also* Kundalini.

Kundalini: (lit. "coiled one") The supreme Power, the primordial Shakti or energy, which lies coiled at the base of the spine, in the muladhara chakra, of every human being. Through initiation, this extremely subtle force is awakened and begins to purify the whole system. As it travels upward through the sushumna nadi, it pierces the various chakras until it finally reaches the sahasrara at the crown of the head. When this happens, the individual self merges into the supreme Self, and the cycle of birth and death comes to an end. *See also* Chakra; Shaktipat.

Kundalini Yoga: The process of attaining union of the individual self with the supreme Self through the evolution of awakened Kundalini energy.

Liberation: Freedom from the cycle of birth and death; the state of realization of oneness with the Absolute. *See also* Enlightenment; Self-realization.

Maharashtra: A state on the west coast of India; the site of Gurumayi's ashram, Gurudev Siddha Peeth. *See also* Ganeshpuri; Gurudev Siddha Peeth.

Maharishi: (lit. "great sage") A term of the highest respect for one who has attained supreme knowledge. Originally found in the law codes of Manu (circa 1200 B.C.), where it refers to the ten Prajapatis, or patriarchs of humanity.

Mahasamadhi: (lit. "the great samadhi") A realized yogi's conscious departure from the body at death.

Mansur Mastana, or *Mansur Al-Hallaj*: (d. circa 922) An ecstatic Sufi poet-saint who lived most of his life in Baghdad. He also journeyed through Iraq, Persia, Gujarat, and Kashmir to the periphery of China. He was hanged as a heretic for his pronouncement *Ana'l Haq*, "I am God."

Mantra: (lit. "that which protects") Sacred words or sounds invested with the power to protect and transform the one who repeats them; the sound-body of God.

Muladhara Chakra: The first psychic center, located at the base of the spine; the resting place of Kundalini before the transmission of Shaktipat. *See also* Chakra; Kundalini.

Nasrudin, Sheik: A figure originating in Turkish folklore during the Middle Ages. He is traditionally used by spiritual teachers to illustrate the antics of the human mind.

Nityananda, Bhagawan: (d. 1961; *Bhagawan*, lit. "the Lord"; *Nityananda*, lit. "eternal bliss") Often referred to by Gurumayi as Bade Baba, Bhagawan Nityananda was Swami Muktananda's Guru and predecessor in the Siddha lineage. He was a born Siddha, living his entire life in the highest state of Consciousness. Little is known of his early life. He came from South India and spent many years traveling in the South, for a time living in a cave not far from Kanhangad.

Later he lived in the sacred region around Mandagni Mountain in Maharashtra, where for centuries sages had performed fire rituals and done austerities. The village of Ganeshpuri grew up around him. Although he rarely spoke, spending many hours in silent ecstasy, thousands of people came to receive his grace. Often their questions were answered, without words, in the stillness of his presence. He left his body on August 8, 1961. Bhagawan Nityananda's samadhi shrine is in the village of Ganeshpuri, a mile from Baba and Gurumayi's ashram, Gurudev Siddha Peeth.

Om or *Aum*: The primal sound, from which the universe emanates; *Om* is the inner essence of all mantras.

Om Namah Shivaya: (lit. "I bow to Shiva") The "five-syllable" Sanskrit mantra of the Siddha lineage, known as the great redeeming mantra because of its power to grant both worldly fulfillment and spiritual realization. In Siddha Yoga, Shiva denotes the inner Self.

Patanjali: The great fourth-century sage and author of the famous *Yoga Sutras*, the exposition of one of the six orthodox philosophies of India. It is the authoritative text of the path of raja yoga. *See also Yoga Sutras*.

Practices: Activities that purify and strengthen the mind and body for the spiritual path; Siddha Yoga practices include chanting, meditation, mantra repetition, hatha yoga, and seva (service). *See also* Sadhana.

Prana: The vital, life-sustaining force of both the individual body and the entire universe.

Pranayama: (lit. "restraining the breath") A yogic technique, consisting of systematic regulation and restraint of the breath, which leads to steadiness of mind.

Pratyabhijnahridayam: (lit. "the heart of the doctrine of recognition") An eleventh-century treatise by Kshemaraja that summarizes the pratyabhijna philosophy of Kashmir Shaivism. It states, in essence, that man has forgotten his true nature by identifying with the body and that realization is a process of recognizing or remembering one's true nature (pratyabhijna), which is the inner Self of supreme bliss and love.

Rama: Seventh incarnation of Vishnu. The story of this divine king and hero is told in the *Ramayana*.

Sadgurunath Maharaj ki Jay!: (lit. "I hail the Master who has revealed the Truth to me!") An exalted expression of gratitude for that which has been received from the Guru. Gurumayi says these words at the beginning and end of every program.

Sadhana: Practices, both physical and mental, on the spiritual path; spiritual discipline.

Sahasrara: The thousand-petaled spiritual center at the crown of the head where one experiences the highest state of Consciousness. *See also* Chakra; Kundalini.

Samadhi: The state of meditative union with the Absolute.

Samadhi Shrine: The final resting place of a great yogi's body. Such shrines are places of worship, permeated with the saint's spiritual power.

Sanskrit: (lit. "perfectly constructed speech") The learned language of India, first found in its ancient form in the Vedas and Upanishads, dating from at least 1200 B.C.; the later language is found in the epics, the *Mahabharata* and the *Ramayana*, starting at 500 B.C. and in other scriptural works like the Puranas. It is said that there are nearly 10,000 inspired Sanskrit works that the pandits, or scholars, of India are able to enumerate.

Self: Divine Consciousness residing in the individual; not different from the supreme Principle.

Self-realization: The state in which the individual ego merges with pure Consciousness.

Shakti: Spiritual power; the divine cosmic Power which, according to Shaivite philosophy, creates and maintains the universe. The immanent aspect of divine Consciousness. *See also* Chiti; Kundalini.

Shaktipat: (lit. "the descent of grace") The transmission of spiritual power or Shakti from the Guru to the disciple; spiritual awakening by grace. *See also* Guru; Kundalini; Shakti.

Shankaracharya: (788-820) The great philosopher-sage who traveled throughout India expounding the teaching of absolute nondualism or Advaita Vedanta, which asserts the identity of the individual soul and the Supreme Soul. In addition to teaching and writing, he established maths, or ashrams, in the four corners of India. The Saraswati Order of monks, to which Baba and Gurumayi belong, was created by Shankaracharya. His written works include *Aparokshanubhuti*, *Atmabodha*, and *Vivekachudamani*.

Shiva: 1) In Shaivism, Supreme Shiva (Paramashiva) is the all-pervasive supreme Reality, and Lord Shiva is the unmoving, transcendent aspect of divine Consciousness. 2) In the Hindu trinity, Shiva is the aspect of God as the destroyer.

Shiva Sutras: A Sanskrit text which Shiva revealed to the ninth-century sage Vasuguptacharya. It consists of seventy-seven sutras, or aphorisms, which according to tradition were found inscribed on a rock in Kashmir. The *Shiva Sutras* are the scriptural authority for the philosophical school known as Kashmir Shaivism. *See also* Kashmir Shaivism.

Siddha: A perfected yogi. One who has attained the state of unity-consciousness, or enlightenment. *See also* Enlightenment; Liberation.

Siddha Guru: A perfected Master who has the power to bestow grace, the inner awakening of divine energy. *See also* Guru; Shaktipat.

Siddha lineage: The unbroken chain of supreme Masters that originates in Lord Shiva. In modern times, the Siddha lineage has passed from Bhagawan Nityananda to Swami Muktananda to Swami Chidvilasananda (Gurumayi). *See also* Nityananda, Bhagawan; Siddha Guru.

Siddha Meditation: Spontaneous meditation based on the awakening of the inner Kundalini energy by a Siddha Master.

Siddha Yoga: The path to union of the individual with the Divine, which begins with Shaktipat, the inner awakening by the grace of a Siddha Guru. Gurumayi is the living Master of this path. Siddha Yoga is also known as the maha yoga, the great yoga, and includes all the branches of yoga.

Siddha Yoga Meditation Center: A place where people gather to practice Siddha Meditation. There are over 600 Siddha Yoga centers around the world.

South Fallsburg, New York: The location of the Siddha Meditation ashram which Baba Muktananda established as the Western headquarters of SYDA Foundation in 1979. Since that time it has expanded to accommodate thousands of visitors who go there to spend time with Gurumayi each summer.

States of Consciousness: The four modes of human experience: waking, dream, deep-sleep, and pure, unchanging awareness. *See also* Turiya.

Sufi: One who practices Sufism, the mystical path of love in the Islamic tradition.

Sufism: The Islamic mystical doctrine that teaches that the goal of life is realization of the divine Principle in the heart.

Sundardas: (1596-1689) A renowned poet-saint born in Rajasthan. The main collection of his Hindi bhajans, or devotional poems, is the *Sundar Granthavati*.

Swami or *Swamiji*: A term of respectful address for a sannyasin, a monk.

Tukaram Maharaj: (1608-1650) A great householder poet-saint of Maharashtra. He received initiation in a dream from his Guru, Babaji, who was a direct spiritual descendent of Jnaneshwar Maharaj. He wrote thousands of abhangas, devotional songs, describing his spiritual experiences, his realization, and the glory of the divine Name.

Turiya: The fourth state of Consciousness, beyond the waking, dream, and deep-sleep states. The turiya state is the state of samadhi, the state of deep meditation.

Upanishads: (lit. "sitting close to") The teachings of the ancient sages of India. The central teaching of the Upanishads is that the Self is the same as Brahman, the Absolute, and the goal of life is the realization of oneness with Brahman. They form the pinnacle of Vedic teachings. *See also* Vedanta.

Vasishtha: Ancient sage and Guru of Lord Rama. The *Yoga Vasishtha*, one of the most important Indian scriptural works, consists of his teachings to Lord Rama.

Vedanta: (lit. "end of the Vedas") One of the six orthodox schools of Indian philosophy, Vedanta was founded by Badarayana. It arose from discussions in the Upanishads about the nature of the Absolute, or the Self, and was systematized by Shankaracharya. *See also* Upanishads.

Vedas: The four ancient, authoritative Hindu scriptures, regarded as divinely revealed. They are the *Rig Veda*, *Yajur Veda*, *Sama Veda*, and *Atharva Veda*.

Vijnana Bhairava: An exposition of the path of yoga based on the principles of Kashmir Shaivism. Originally composed in Sanskrit, probably in the seventh century, this text describes 112 dharanas, or centering exercises, that can give the immediate experience of union with God.

Yoga: (lit. "union") The state of oneness with the Self, with God; the practices leading to that state.

Yoga Sutras: The basic scripture of the path of raja yoga, the *Yoga Sutras* are a collection of aphorisms written in Sanskrit by Patanjali in the fourth century. He expounds different methods for the attainment of the state of yoga, or samadhi, in which the movement of the mind ceases, and the Witness rests in its own bliss. *See also* Patanjali.

Yogi: One who practices yoga; also, one who has attained perfection through yogic practices. *See also* Yoga.

FURTHER READING

By Gurumayi Chidvilasananda

Ashes At My Guru's Feet

Kindle My Heart, Volumes I & II

By Swami Muktananda

From the Finite to the Infinite, Volumes I & II

I Am That

Play of Consciousness

Kundalini: The Secret of Life

Secret of the Siddhas

Siddha Meditation

I Have Become Alive

Does Death Really Exist?

Where Are You Going?

Light on the Path

The Perfect Relationship

Mukteshwari I & II

Satsang With Baba, Volumes I-V

Reflections of the Self

In the Company of a Siddha

Mystery of the Mind

Getting Rid of What You Haven't Got

I Love You

To Know the Knower

The Self Is Already Attained

A Book for the Mind

I Welcome You All With Love

God Is With You

References

Hariharananda. *The Yoga Philosophy of Patanjali*. Albany, New York: SUNY Press, 1983.

Kshemaraja. *The Doctrine of Recognition: A Translation of* Pratyabhijnahridayam. Translated with an Introduction and Notes by Jaideva Singh. Albany, New York: SUNY Press, 1990.

Radhakrishnan, S., trans. *Bhagavad Gita*. New York: Harper & Row, 1973.

Radhakrishnan, S., ed. *The Principal Upanishads*. London: George Allen & Unwin Ltd., 1974.

Sadananda. *Vedantasara*. Edited by Swami Nikhilananda. Mayavati, India: Advaita Ashram, 1974.

Shankaracharya, *Atmabodha* [Self-knowledge]. Translated with comments and notes by Swami Nikhilananda. New York: Ramakrishna-Vivekananda Center, 1970.

Shankaracharya, *Vivekachudamani* [The Crest Jewel of Discrimination]. Mayavati, India: Advaita Ashram, 1974.

Singh, Jaideva, trans. *Shiva Sutras*. Delhi, India. Motilal Banarsidass, 1979.

Singh, Jaideva, trans. *The Yoga of Delight, Wonder, and Astonishment: A Translation of the* Vijnana-bhairava. Albany, New York: SUNY Press, 1991.

Vasishtha, *The Concise Yoga Vasishtha*. Translated by Swami Venkatesananda. Albany, New York: SUNY Press, 1984.

INDEX